Leadership –
By The Book

with illustrations by the author

David M. Atkinson

Printed in the United States of America by

Faith
BAPTIST CHURCH
PUBLICATIONS & PRINTING

Faith Baptist Church Publications
Fort Pierce, FL 34982
www.fbcpublications.com

Dedication

—༺༻—

I dedicate this book to the followers in the four churches I have pastored, the followers who have let me lead. Without followers, there are no leaders.

Note: Reference to an individual should not be construed as an endorsement of all of the conduct, views or associations of that individual. Reference to a book, essay or article should not be construed as an endorsement of all the contents of that book or article or of everything the author ever wrote or did.

Acknowledgements

—ᴠᴠ—

I make few claims to originality for this book and wish to acknowledge my indebtedness to those leaders, past and present, whose examples have been such good teachers. There is more about leadership that I do not know than I do know. My thirty-year study of the subject leaves me still fascinated with its intricacies, conundrums and variations.

Christian leadership is a delicate synthesis of "grace and truth" (John 1:17). So there are times when the principles of leadership may seem to contradict each other. At such times we would do well to remember that every coin has two sides and that it is always context that recommends what is the course of wisdom at any given moment.

I am grateful to Robert M. Strozier whose article featuring several quotes from great military generals sparked what has become for me a lifelong captivation.

I am also deeply grateful to my wife, Jane, who managed to squeeze the typesetting of this book into her busy schedule as a Pastor's wife, full time medical transcriptionist, church nursery worker, mother ... and grandmother. Her self-discipline leaves me in awe.

A number of the illustrations I use are taken from Paul Lee Tan's magnificent *Encyclopedia of 7700 Illustrations.* That book is a goldmine for writers and speakers.

- David M. Atkinson
April, 2007

"Stonewall!"

—ᴍ—

Listen, all who talk of heroes,
Gather 'round and let me tell
A story 'bout a hero
Who was brave and fought right well.

Though some cadets dubbed him "Tom Fool,"
And others called him "Old Jack,"
His steel blue-gray eyes would stare
'Til those cadets felt the flack.

Our man's name was Thomas Jackson
And he taught at Lexington –
Way down in old Virginy
Where the cotton kissed the sun.

It was in the eighteen-fifties
He was prof at V.M.I. –
Optics and philosophy –
This killjoy hick made them sigh

'Cause if they asked him a question
He'd just back up, read again.
So they said that he was dumb
And made noise and raised some Cain.

continued

But our friend, Thomas, was no fool –
Just a man not yet in place –
And always at the table
He would bow and say a grace.

Now this Jackson was a church man,
But some said, "Among the quacks!"
When on Lord's Day afternoons
He held Sunday School for blacks.

So when he donned Confed'rate gray
It was no remark on race.
'Twas just ol' Virginy's "right"
To tend her own hard case.

July twenty-one, sixty-one –
Lord's Day sticky with the sun –
The Rebels met the Fed'rals
Near a poor creek called Bull Run.

Washington, thirty miles away
Took on gay, spectator mood.
Congressmen, wives and vendors
Traveled down and gawked there rude.

They'd see them gray-coats put to flight,
Their blue boys move on Richmond.
They would give those Rebs a run.
They would see them whipped, out-gunned.

A major's sword now raised aloft
Waved his regiment forward.
A frightened 'Bama boy tried
But his feet took him backward

And his dry mouth fell to a gape.
His voice cried, "Momma, momma!"
And in terror could not stop
So its last word was "Momma!"

Tom Jackson paced there on his mount –
(Little Sorrel sure was short.)
They seemed to look mismatched through
The smoke of the guns' retort.

But one thing now was very clear –
The man they had called "Tom Fool"
Who couldn't keep one class in line –
An entire brigade could rule.

Tom always looked for the high ground
And he spied him Henry Hill.
To that hill he resorted
And watched with an iron will.

Then midst the sweat and dirt and blood
An officer called through din,
"Gen'ral, the day's against us."
Said Tom with an almost grin,

"If you think so, Sir, don't say so.
You just keep it to yourself."
"General, they beat us back."
"Give 'em bayonet for pelf!"

The blue line came up Henry Hill
And Jackson's left arm came down.
Then old First Brigade let fire.
The Feds' flags fell to the ground.

continued

When General Bee looked he saw
The Virgin'ians proud and tall.
So he yelled to his Rebs, "There
Jackson stands like a stone wall!"

Thomas J. Jackson was no fool
For he won the fight that day.
Virginy sparked the Rebels
And ... "Stonewall!" the folks still say.

- David M. Atkinson
October 24, 1994

The Author's Foreword

—⁂—

We have a serious problem in the Western world. The problem is the scarcity of leadership. In Act I, Scene II of Shakespeare's Julius Caesar, the bard has Cassius describe Caesar as follows:

> "Why, man, he doth bestride the narrow world
> Like a Colossus, and we petty men now
> Walk under his huge legs and peep about
> To find ourselves dishonorable graves."

I am far from being alone in my lament over the lack of leadership. In the *Toronto Star* on August 12, 1978, Gordon Legge asked, "Is there anyone out there to lead us?" The August 6, 1979, issue of *Newsweek* asked, "Where Have All The Heroes Gone?" In 1981 Jossey Bass Publishers of San Francisco and London released Arthur Levine's book which was entitled, *When Dreams and Heroes Died.*

We are left with a longing like the one expressed in *A Man* by Stephen Phillips:

> O for a living man to lead!
> That will not babble when we bleed;
> And one that in a nation's night

Hath solitary certitude of light.

But Phillips not only diagnoses the problem. He at least hints at the solution. What we need is light. This book dares to suggest that the light we need is the Light that guided civilization for centuries – until the blighting frosts of rationalism, the Age of Enlightenment, higher criticism and humanism began to extinguish it. I speak of the Bible.

Sir Walter Scott was the celebrated author of *The Waverly* novels and when Scott was dying, he said to his son-in-law, Lockhart, "Bring me the book."

Lockhart asked, "Which book?"

Sir Walter Scott replied, "There is but one book – the Bible."

Each year new books on leadership appear on the shelves of both secular and Christian bookstores. Many of them are helpful and informative and will stand the test of time. Some of them are trendy and faddish and will be relegated to the bottom of the box as the dated musings of yesterday's gurus.

The greatest book ever written on the subject of leadership is the Bible. The Bible was inspired by the Holy Spirit of God and recorded by about 39 or 40 authors over a span of about 1550 years. This is the span of sixty generations.

Sixty generations are sufficient time to include – at least in type or kind – every situation and scenario that every leader will ever face.

The years come and go. The weaponry becomes more sophisticated. The technology advances. Men and women become more clever sinners.

However, the basic problems of human interaction remain the same. The faces change. The times and places change, but crisis, challenge, conflict and opportunity speak virtually the same lines as they keep marching across the stage of human history.

This little book proposes to examine leadership by **the** Book. It is my prayer that this small contribution to the literary scene will cause readers who are familiar with the Bible to apply its principles to life and leadership as never before. And I dare to hope that readers hitherto unfamiliar with the Bible will be moved to secure a copy and allow it to become the source of personal conversion, wisdom, guidance and genius that it has been for millions.

In communicating with General Bertrand on the island of St. Helena, no less a leader than Napoleon Bonaparte said in 1816:

The Gospel is not a book; it is a Living Creature, with an action, a power, which conquers everything that opposes its extension.

Behold it upon this table, this book surpassing all others (here the Emperor solemnly placed his hand upon it): I never omit to read it, and every day with new pleasure.

Nowhere is to be found such a series of beautiful ideas, and admirable moral maxims, which pass before us like the battalions of a celestial army ... The soul can never go astray with this book for its guide.

Christ proved that He was the Son of the Eternal by His disregard of time. All His doctrines signify one only and the same thing – eternity. What a proof of the divinity of Christ!

If you [General Bertrand] do not perceive that Jesus Christ is God, very well: then I did wrong to make you general.[1]

In a discussion with Count de Motholon Napoleon stated:

I know men, and I tell you that Jesus Christ is not a man. Superficial minds see a resemblance between Christ and the founders of empires, and the gods of other religions. That resemblance does not exist.

There is between Christianity and whatever other religions the distance of infinity ...[2]

The cover of this book features William L. Maughan's masterpiece portrait of Thomas J. "Stonewall" Jackson kneeling in prayer while he holds a small copy of the New Testament. The life, leadership and military tactics of the brilliant Confederate general have been studied around the world. Young Tom Jackson acquired his first Bible when he was just a teenager. One of Jackson's first purchases after his open profession of faith was a copy of the New Testament. It became the family Bible, replete with birth and death dates. Jackson read it daily and underlined a number of passages. Two appear to have become favorites that brought him comfort in time of tragedy: Revelation 21:4 and Romans 8:28.

Jackson scrutinized all of the major military campaigns recounted in the Old Testament.

When he started a Sunday School for blacks in the autumn of 1855, according to J. Cleveland Cady, some of the Bourbon aristocracy of Lexington, Virginia, criticized, taunted and scorned him. He was even threatened with prosecution. But Jackson "paid them no mind" and continued leading his eager charges in Bible readings and simple Bible instruction. On the first Sunday of each month, Testaments and Bibles were awarded to those who had shown outstanding progress. Enrollment in the class eventually reached from eighty to over 100 people of all ages.

Jackson read the Bible from cover to cover many times and grouped scores of biblical passages under headings such as "Love of God in Christ ..." and "Purification through the righteousness of Christ." He taught a Sunday morning Bible class in addition to the afternoon class for blacks.

It was his custom to read the Bible first during his study time which followed the 11 a.m. close of his second lecture at Virginia Military Institute. His library had military treatises on Caesar, Washington, Napoleon and ... five Bibles! These included translations in French, Spanish and Greek. His desk was a high one which required that he stand all the time. He had it made to order.

When Jackson was dying he asked Lieutenant James Smith, one of his attendants, if he knew where the Bible gives generals a model for their official reports of battles. Smith laughed and confessed he had never studied the Bible in that light. Jackson pointed Smith to the narrative of Joshua's battles with the Amalekites. A model of "clearness, brevity and modesty," he called it. "One that traced the victory to the right source, the blessing of God."[5]

When he was even closer to "crossing over," Smith quoted Romans 8:28 to him. Jackson responded, "Yes. That's it! That's it!"

Jackson, like Sir Walter Scott and Napoleon Bonaparte, was a man of "the Book."

And thousands of other successful leaders have emulated him in this regard. If we live by the Book, we lead and conquer the eternal way. If we disregard the principles of the Bible, its Gospel conquers us. We forfeit leadership.

David M. Atkinson
Rosewood House
Dyer, Indiana, 2007

What Great Leaders Have Said About "The Book"

—ɯɯ—

George Washington said, "It is impossible to rightly govern the world without God and the Bible."

Our third President, Thomas Jefferson, said, "The Bible makes the best people in the world."

Our sixth President, John Quincy Adams, said, "So great is my veneration of the Bible, that the earlier my children begin to read it the more confident will be my hope that they will prove useful citizens of their country and respectable members of society."

On May 29, 1845, our seventh President, Andrew Jackson, said, "The Bible is true. I have tried to conform to its spirit as near as possible. Upon that sacred volume I rest my hope for eternal salvation; through the merits and blood of our blessed Lord and Savior, Jesus Christ." He also said, "That book, sir, is the rock on which our republic rests."

Our twelfth President, Zachary Taylor, said, "It was for love of the truths of this great Book (the Bible) that our fathers abandoned their native shores for the wilderness."

Our sixteenth President, Abraham Lincoln, said, "In regards to this great Book, I have but to say it is the best gift God has given to man. All the good the Savior gave to the world was communicated through this book."

Our 28th President, Theodore Roosevelt, said, "To every man who faces life with real desire to do his part in everything, I appeal for a study of the Bible."

Our 34th President, Dwight Eisenhower, said, "The Bible is endorsed by the ages. Our civilization is built upon its words. In no other book is there such a collection of inspired wisdom, reality and hope." He also said, "To read the Bible is to take a trip to a fair land where the spirit is strengthened and faith renewed." And in 1954, President Eisenhower said, "The purpose of a devout and united people was set forth in the pages of the Bible ... (1) to live in freedom, (2) to work in a prosperous land ... and (3) to obey the commandments of God ... This Biblical story of the Promised Land inspired the founders of America. It continues to inspire us."

Our fortieth President, Ronald Reagan, said, "Within the covers of the Bible are all the answers for all the problems men face. The Bible can touch hearts, order minds and refresh souls."

Queen Victoria in a message to an African prince said, "Tell your prince that this Book (the Bible) is the secret of England's greatness."

Horace Greeley said, "It is impossible to mentally or socially enslave a Bible-reading people. The principles of the Bible are the groundwork of human freedom."

President Woodrow Wilson said, "I ask every man and woman in this audience that from this day on they will realize that part of the destiny of America lies in their daily perusal of this great Book."

General Douglas MacArthur said, "Believe me, sir, never a night goes by, be I ever so tired, but I read the Word of God before I go to bed."

President Herbert Hoover said, "The whole of the inspiration of our civilization springs from the teachings of Christ and the lessons of the Prophets. To read the Bible for these fundamentals is a necessity of American life."

Charles Dickens said, "The New Testament is the very best book that ever was or ever will be known in the world."

Robert G. Lee, three-time President of the Southern Baptist Convention and Pastor of the Bellevue Baptist Church of Memphis, Tennessee, wrote:

"The Bible is the Word of God. Inexhaustive in its adequacy, It is harmonious in infinite complexity. Supernatural in origin. Unique in authorship. Human in penmanship. Infallible in authority. Infinite in scope. Universal in interest. Eternal in duration. Personal in application. Regenerative in power. Immortal in its hopes. Immeasurable in influence. Inspired in totality … the miracle book of diversity in unity. There is not a sin it does not condemn, not a virtue it fails to mention. It is an oasis in a desert of despair. This wonderful book travels more highways, walks more bypaths, knocks at more doors, speaks to more people in their mother tongue than any book ever printed."

Part I

LEADERSHIP IS ...

Queen Victoria (1819 – 1901)

This magnificent lady was queen of Great Britain and Ireland from 1837 – 1901. Her reign was the longest in British history. When, at 4 years of age, little Victoria was told that she would be queen some day, she replied, "I will be a good one." At 16 she wrote in her journal, "I went to St. James Palace with the firm determination to become a true Christian." While many of her subjects were tormented by doubts about the Bible or were turning their backs on Christianity, Victoria clung to a simple but deeply held religious belief. It was said that the sun never set upon her empire.

Robert G. Lee (1886 - 1978)

The gentleman-orator of the Southern Baptist Convention was raised on a farm and had early pastorates in South Carolina. He became pastor of the Bellevue Baptist Church in Memphis, Tennessee, in 1927 and continued until 1960 when he was elected Pastor Emeritus. He served three terms as President of the Southern Baptist Convention, preached his signature sermon, "Pay Day – Some Day," over 700 times and received 23,721 new members into Bellevue during his ministry of 33 years.

Margaret Thatcher (1925 -)

The Iron Lady of 20th century British politics was leader of the Conservative party for 15 years. She became Prime Minister of Great Britain in 1979, the first woman to hold this position. She led with dignity over a span of eleven turbulent years. No prime minister of modern times sought to change Britain and its place in the world as drastically as she did. She was a strong nationalist and looked with suspicion upon the internationalism of the European Union. She said, "The twin, opposing temptations of statesmen are hubris and timidity … but what is morally right often turns out to be politically expedient."

Leadership is ... Obvious

—ɯ—

Prime Minister Margaret Thatcher said, "Being a leader is a lot like being a lady. If you have to tell people you are one, you aren't."

We may not always be able to say what leadership is but we know it when we see it. General Douglas MacArthur of World War II renown is one of the most unforgettable examples of the obvious nature of leadership.

When President Harry Truman relieved MacArthur of his command in the Far East, nearly 250,000 Japanese standing 10 deep had risen before 6:28 a.m. on April 16, 1951, to line the twelve miles to the airport. They were held in check by 10,000 Japanese policemen. Some held banners, "We love you, MacArthur," "With Deep Regret" and "We are grateful to the General."

When General MacArthur's plane touched down at Hickam Field in Hawaii, a crowd estimated by *The New York Times* at 100,000 was waiting.

As the General touched down at San Francisco, he put his hands on his son's shoulders and said, "Well, my boy, we're home." A half-million people were in the streets yelling, fainting and blocking the motorcade route. It took the General's party 20 minutes just to reach the cars and two hours to crawl 14 miles. The following morning another half million hurrahed as he rode through the downtown area.

When his plane arrived at Washington National Airport after midnight on April 19, 12,000 people were milling around outside the terminal. When he addressed the House of Representatives, his 34 minute address was interrupted by 30 ovations. When he had finished his speech he handed his manuscript to the clerk, waved to his wife Jean, and stepped down into pandemonium. The legislators were sobbing their praise, struggling to touch his sleeve, all but prostrating themselves in his path. In New York Herbert Hoover called MacArthur "a reincarnation of St. Paul into a great General of the army who came out of the East." Cheeks were wet, voices hoarse, chests heaving.

When the MacArthurs checked into the Waldorf Astoria Hotel in New York City, 150,000 letters and 20,000 telegrams awaited them with more pouring in "by the sackload." When he rode through Manhattan the next morning several million people - including 40,000 longshoremen who had walked off their jobs to be there - lined the streets. It took nearly seven hours for the motorcade to cover the 19.2 mile route. Over 2,859 tons of ticker tape and liter were dumped on the motorcade.

In Chicago three million people lined the 23 mile parade route to Soldier Field, and he, Jean and Arthur were showered with $5,000 worth of orchids. In little Murfreesboro, Tennessee, which had been Jean's home for 34 years, 50,000 people welcomed him. In Boston another half million stood and watched his car go by.

Years later, in July, 1961, when Douglas MacArthur returned to Manila to help the Filipinos celebrate the 15th anniversary of their liberation from Japan, two million Filipinos lined the motorcade route and the band played, "Old Soldiers Never Die." The leadership of Douglas MacArthur was obvious.

Of the Duke of Wellington, after he defeated Napoleon at the Battle of Waterloo, Lord Uxbridge said, "I thought I had heard enough of this man, but he has far surpassed my expectations. It is not a man but a god."

The August 6, 1979, issue of *Newsweek* magazine featured a sketch of Teddy Roosevelt leading the charge up San Juan Hill and asked this question, "Where have all the heroes gone?" It was obvious to the editors of *Newsweek* that Roosevelt was a leader.

The August 12, 1978 *Toronto Star* ran pictures of Winston Churchill, Charles de Gaulle and Franklin D. Roosevelt and asked, **"Is there anyone out there to lead us?"** The article quoted Warren Bennis as saying, "True leaders today are an endangered species because of the whirl of events and circumstances beyond rational control."

Douglas MacArthur (1880 - 1964)

No American general ever stirred the passions of followship the way this soldier did. William Manchester called him, "The American Caesar." He was the leading American general of both World War II and the Korean War. When President Franklin Roosevelt ordered him and his family to leave the Philippines for their own safety, he sent the famous three word message, "I shall return," back from Australia. And return he did! He and his father were the only father-son combination to both receive the prestigious Medal of Honor.

Leadership is ... Confounding

—⚹—

What is your concept of a leader? What would your sketch look like if you were asked to draw a picture of an ideal leader? How do you picture the ideal leader in your mind? Is he or she tall or short, black or white, telegenic or rugged, aloof or warm and approachable? Is he talkative or "the strong, silent type?" Does he lead because he is a "great communicator," or is it his "leadership style" and personna that carry the day?

If you would have trouble doing this assignment, you get 100 marks and a gold star! If you are thinking, "I really couldn't do that because there *is* *no* typical leader," you anticipated my opinion perfectly.

There really is no such creature as the "typical leader."

Columbus was the son of a weaver, and a weaver himself. Homer was the son of a small farmer. Terence was a slave. Oliver Cromwell was the son of a London brewer.

Daniel Defoe was a hostler and a son of a butcher. Whitefield was the son of an innkeeper at Gloucester. Virgil was the son of a porter. Horace was the son of a shopkeeper. Shakespeare was the son of a woodstapler. Milton was the son of a money-scrivener. Robert Burns was a plowman in Ayrshire.

God likes to use the unlikely so only He gets the glory.

Napoleon, descendant of an obscure family of Corsica, was a major when he married Josephine, the daughter of a tobacconist, Creole of Martinique. Catherine, Empress of Russia, was a camp-grisette. Cincinnatus was plowing in his vineyard when the dictatorship of Rome was offered him. Abraham Lincoln was a rail-splitter.

Gladstone gave no evidence of unusual ability as a boy. Napoleon stood 42nd in his class at the military academy, (but who ever heard of the other 41?) Patrick Henry was a lazy boy, uninterested in study. He failed at business, at farming, and again in business. Then he tried law, and American history tells the rest of the story.

Henry Ward Beecher, the popular Congregational preacher, as a boy, was a "poor writer, a miserable speller, with a thick utterance and a bashful reticence which people took for stolid stupidity." Booker T. Washington was born a slave, had an early life of most unusual struggle and became one of the most valued educators of his time.

Shakespeare held horses at the door of a London theater before he held the attention of all ages. The shoemaker's last would have been the most appropriate coat of arms for William Carey, the missionary.

A barbershop was the starting place of Copernicus. In 1869 H. J. Heinz planted a small plot of horseradish. He and two women and a boy grated and bottled the root. J.L.

Kraft was a grocery clerk who started with a capital of $65 to peddle cheese from a one-horse wagon.

John Wanamaker was the son of a brick maker. Sir John McDonald, Canada's greatest statesman, was the son of a plain Scottish storekeeper.

> It doesn't take a man of giant mold
> To cast a giant shadow on the wall;
> But he who in our daily sight
> Seems but a figure mean and small,
> Outlined in fame's illusive light
> May cast a silhouette sublime
> Across the canvas of our time.
>
> — Unknown

God likes to surprise us when He picks His leaders!

Young Thomas Edison came home from school one day with a note pinned on him. The note from his teacher read, "Keep this boy at home. He is too stupid to learn." The United States Patent Office granted him 1,098 patents – 122 of them before he was thirty years of age. "Work heals and ennobles," he said on his 75th birthday.

The great evangelist, Dwight L. Moody, was refused membership by several New England churches. They apparently thought he wasn't ready!

On May 2, 1888, the young man who later became the world-renown biblical expositor, G. Campbell Morgan, was rejected for ordination to the Methodist ministry at Lichfield Road Church, Birmingham, England. Morgan sent a one-word wire to his father, who was also a minister, "Rejected!"

His father wired back, "Rejected on earth. Accepted in heaven."

An expert said of famous football coach Vince Lombardi, "He possesses minimal football knowledge. Lacks motivation."

Louisa May Alcott, the author of *Little Women*, was advised by her family to find work as a servant or seamstress.

Beethoven handled the violin awkwardly and preferred playing his own compositions instead of improving his technique. His teacher called him hopeless as a composer.

The teacher of famous opera singer Enrico Caruso said Caruso had no voice at all and could not sing.

Walt Disney was fired by a newspaper for lacking ideas. He also went bankrupt several times before he built Disneyland.

Alfred Tennyson's grandfather gave him 10 shillings for writing an eulogy on his grandmother. Handing it to the lad the old man said, "There, that is the first money you ever earned by your poetry, and take my word for it, it will be the last."

Benjamin Franklin's mother-in-law hesitated at letting her daughter marry a printer. There were already two printing offices in the United States, and she feared that the country might not be able to support a third.

Here's how *The Chicago Times* in 1865 evaluated Lincoln's Gettysburg Address in commenting on it the day after its delivery: "The cheek of every American must tingle with shame as he reads the silly, flat, and dish-watery utterances of a man who has to be pointed out to intelligent foreigners as President of the United States."

Randolph Churchill seriously berated and sadly under-rated and neglected his young son, Winston.

The father of Gladys Harding of Abilene, Kansas, said to Gladys one day, "Get rid of that Eisenhower kid. He'll never amount to anything." Well, *both* Gladys and Ike *did*. Gladys *did* get rid of Ike, and Ike *did* go on to amount to something – President of the USA. It is to be hoped that Mr. Harding was not in the prophecy business!

In 1 Corinthians 1:26-29 the apostle Paul wrote, "For ye see your calling, brethren, how that not many wise men after the flesh, not many mighty, not many noble, are called: but God hath chosen the foolish things of the world to confound the wise; and God hath chosen the weak things of the world to confound the things which are mighty ... and things which are despised, hath God chosen ... that no flesh should glory in His [God's] presence."

God chooses the Joshuas - and the Deborahs, the Aquillas - and the Priscillas, the Timothys - and the Loises.

- Both Napoleon Bonaparte and Winston Churchill were very short.

- Ludwig von Beethoven and Thomas Edison were deaf.

- Helen Keller was both blind and deaf.

- Lord Byron had a club foot.

- Robert Louis Stevenson and John Keats had tuberculosis.

- William Wilberforce and Alexander Pope were hunchbacks.

- Admiral Nelson only had one eye.

- Fanny Crosby and George Matheson were blind.

- William Cowper was manic depressive and suicidal.

- Julius Caesar was an epileptic.

- Peter Stuyvesant had a wooden leg.

- And journalist George Will made a good case for our seeing Franklin Delano Roosevelt's polio as *the* thing that made FDR so "broadly empathetic" to the needs and hurts of people that he was returned to the presidency more times than any other American.

So, at the outset, let us remember that God is not the God of the stereotypical. He is the God of surprising and infinite variety. He just loves to use a David when all of us are focused on Eliab. Goliath was 9.75 feet tall. King Saul was probably looking for a man 9.8 feet tall to fit his humanistic computation of what it would take to conquer Goliath! David at this time was probably between 5 and 6 feet tall.

Let us also remember that there is another Leader who towers infinitely above the heads of all other leaders. He, too, had an unlikely start. He was born in a stable.

One night when he was chatting with a group of friends, the literary giant Charles Lamb boiled the whole thing down to its bottom-line implication. Said Lamb, "If Alexander the Great or Charlemagne or Napoleon were to come into the room, we would all stand up out of respect. If Jesus Christ walked in, we would fall on our faces in adoration."

The greatest leader who ever walked on earth was Jesus Christ.

Leadership Is ... Character Superior To Your Circumstances

—ɯ—

In his book *Stonewall Jackson*, Allen Tate writes, "Great leaders have character superior to their circumstances," and declares that Jackson was such a man.

After God Himself, **the greatest security a man has is his own character. Character preserves a leader.** It is what causes a leader to "come back" after an apparently fatal blow. This is a law of sowing and reaping. You can't keep a *good* man down for long. Goodness will prevail.

Our English word "character" comes from the Greek word meaning "expression of." We *are* what we do.

Proverbs 23:7 says, "For as he thinketh in his heart, so is he."

Heraclitus said, "A man's character is his fate."

Fred Smith wrote, "Leadership is something you are and something you do."

Booker T. Washington said, "Character is power."

Lack of character translates into foibles at the precise moment when consistency is required.

Albert Einstein wrote, "Try not to become a man of success, but rather try to become a man of value."

Ralph Waldo Emerson wrote, "The character of the leader determines the character of his organization."

Robert Schmidgall observed, "We teach what we know; we reproduce what we are."

General Omar Bradley said, "The world has achieved brilliance without conscience. Ours is a world of nuclear giants and ethical infants." Joe Collins wrote of the "deep-seated integrity" of General Bradley.

While addressing a group of bankers in Rockport, Maine, General Norman Schwarzkopf said, "When placed in command – take charge. Do what's right, not what you think the high headquarters wants or what you think will make you look good." He also said, "There is no such thing as a born leader ... Most great leaders are ordinary people thrust into extraordinary circumstances."

Douglas Southall Freeman insisted that General Robert E. Lee was a totally uncomplicated man. He was speaking of Lee's transparency of intent and character. Even Thomas Connelly who seems to think that his calling was to debunk "the Lee myth" grudgingly admits, "Robert E. Lee was a good man whose qualities often far transcended the pettiness of many who surrounded him in the Civil War years. No one would question that he was a man of grace, dignity, humility and deep religious convictions ... Much of his greatness may have been due to his ability to control the elements of frustration, self-doubt and unhappiness which troubled his life."

Self-control is indeed one of the hallmarks of character. Galatians 5:23 lists "temperance" or self-control or continence as one aspect of the fruit of the Holy Spirit.

Robert E. Lee's diary contains long notations on child rearing. He emphasized the need "not only to make the child obey externally but internally to make the obedience sincere and hearty." He said, "Cultivate in the child's mind a love of candor, straight-forwardness, integrity, along with a corresponding hatred of falsehood ... The cultivation must be by the training of motive and principles into confirmed habits."

Stanley Horn was asked why General Lee had become a national symbol since "the fame of but few soldiers has survived such failures as he experienced." Horn replied that "the answer was not in his soldiery, but in his character which demonstrated the greatness of steadiness, of such high ideals and principles that his whole conduct was governed by them."

John Locke said, "The actions of men are the best interpreters of their thoughts."

Harold Kohn said, "Brooks become crooked from taking the path of least resistance. So do people."

Bob Jones, Sr. said, "Do right till the stars fall."

What we long for reveals what we really are.

Woodrow Wilson remarked, "Time after time Robert E. Lee was offered opportunities to gain fame and wealth, but neither factor influenced his decision to take a course of action he conscientiously believed to be right."

The British statesman George Canning said, "My road must be through character to power; I will try no other course; and I am sanguine enough to believe that this course though not perhaps the quickest, is the surest."[9]

Os Guinness writes, "Character was traditionally understood as the inner form that makes anyone or anything what it is ... It is therefore deeper than, and different from, such outer concepts as personality, image, reputation and celebrity. Character was ... the core reality in which thoughts, words, decisions, behavior and relationships are rooted ... Character determined behavior ... Character was who we are when no one sees us – but God."[9]

In the eyes of Stonewall Jackson nothing more disqualified someone than a defect in character.

Colin Coote, the British journalist wrote, "Though (Winston) Churchill never disinclined to take office, a refusal to compromise in order to get it kept him out of it for eleven years; and if it be objected that he has often changed his party, I would be prepared to argue that the changes have been only to suit (his) unchanging views."

Peter Kuzmic said, "Charisma without character leads to catastrophe."

Character flaws and foibles can be fatal.

Eisenhower studied and worked in the attic of his quarters in the Command School at Fort Leavenworth in 1925 and 1926. When the term ended and the ratings were posted, Maj. Dwight Eisenhower stood No. 1 in the class of 275 officers.

One of the instructors at that Command School was an officer named George S. Patton, Jr. He made a remark to Eisenhower the day the rankings were announced. That night, bursting with jubilance, Eisenhower repeated it to Mamie.

"Here's a big laugh, Mamie," he said. "This fellow George Patton, you know, the instructor, he came up to me and congratulated me and do you know what he said? He said, 'Major, some day I'll be working for you.' How's that for a laugh?"[6]

It is almost universally acknowledged that General Patton was a brilliant and tenacious military strategist. How tragic it is that Patton's authoritarian temper and lack of self-control kept him from rising as high in leadership as he might have! He might have become Supreme Commander of the Allied forces in Europe and, perhaps President of the United States, had he not been his own worst enemy. As it turned out both of these positions fell to General Dwight D. Eisenhower, the soldier who couched his authority in an infectious grin.

The essence of Patton's foible is embodied in two infamous incidents where he slapped American soldiers in a fit of rage. A memoir written by Patton's former cavalry commander, Maj. Gen. Kenyon A. Joyce, contains the record of Patton's own word-for-word confession. Patton said:

"In both instances, the action was inexcusable on my part ... There is no real extenuation but I will tell you what happened in one of the cases ... I visited an (American field) hospital where there were a number of badly wounded … (Then I came to) a man sitting on the side of his bunk, not bandaged or showing any signs of medical care that had been in such tragic evidence all down the ward. I approached him and said, 'What happened to you, my man? Did you get wounded?' He looked like a cowardly rat and whined like one. Coming on top of the wonderful courage and great spirit I had seen displayed by other men in the ward, it caused a consuming revulsion to come over me.

"I stepped closer to this supine creature, told him to get up on his feet and try to act like a soldier. I then asked him if the example of those brave men in the ward did not stir up something in him that would make him want to do his part. He said, 'Ah, no, those guys don't mean nothing. I just can't take it.'

"With that, something burst in me. I said, 'You rat' and slapped him across the face with my gloves, turned on my heel and walked away. It was inexcusable on my part. I was a fool but the contrast between those brave men of valor and this creeping thing did something to me. The other case (on August 10) was somewhat similar and in that I was equally a fool."

In November of 1943 Drew Pearson told the story on his weekly syndicated radio program. Some congressmen and senators demanded Patton's dismissal. Eisenhower had to make a difficult decision. Eisenhower decided that he would not sack Patton completely because the cause needed him. However, Eisenhower also decided that Patton would never rise any higher in the chain of command. Patton had revealed his own ceiling level. Eisenhower decided that henceforth his criterion for the highest commands would be conscientious mediocrity rather than tactical brilliance marred by temperamental outbursts.

Privately Patton criticized Eisenhower for not coming out in support of him. Carlo D'Este writes, "What (Patton) could not, and never did comprehend, was that he could not simply say 'I'm sorry' and expect that he could carry on as if nothing had ever happened. His punishment was far more than exile in Palermo for the foreseeable future: It was to be the denial of an army group command in the decisive campaigns of World War II."

Patton went from commanding 240,000 men to less than 5,000. His critics were sarcastically inverting his vainglorious nickname by calling him, "Our blood, his Guts." Eisenhower seems to have privately agreed with them. Butcher wrote, "(Ike) thinks Patton would prefer the war to go on if it meant further aggrandizement for him. Neither does he mind sacrificing lives if by so doing he can gain greater fame." It was a reflection of Patton's obsession with carving his place in history that even his closest friend viewed him as intrinsically a glory hound. Or, as Eisenhower's biographer Piers Brendon has less charitably written: "Ike recognized that Patton's vicious and manic qualities were better calculated to win victories than the sober virtues of less inspired generals."[7]

Dwight D. Eisenhower (1890 - 1969)

Born and raised the son of humble Mennonite pacifists, the boy with the infectious and disarming grin was destined for greatness. He attended West Point and later entered the Command School at Fort Leavenworth in 1925. He studied there in the attic of his quarters. When his final term ended in 1926, the Major stood #1 in a class of 275 officers. In 1943 he was appointed Supreme Commander of the Allied Forces in Europe. Unpossessed of the dynamic charisma of General George Patton, "Ike" had staying power and went on to become a two term President of the United States.

Leadership Is ... Servanthood

—◊◊◊—

The *Bits and Pieces* newsletter said, "The trouble with being a leader today is that you can't be sure whether people are following you or ... chasing you."

Leadership is a stewardship (responsibility or guardianship) of influence which the sovereign God gives to an obedient and faithful servant.

Several biblical passages suggest various elements of this definition of leadership. We here mention several of them.

Psalm 75:5-7, "Lift not up your horn on high: speak not with a stiff neck. For *promotion cometh neither from the east, nor from the west, nor from the south. But God* is the judge: he *putteth down one, and setteth up another.*"

In his largely self-serving memoirs dictated on the island of St. Helena at the end of his life, a weakened and sickly Napoleon said, "For all that I held the rudder, the waves were a good deal stronger. I was never in truth my own master; I was always governed by circumstances."

Matthew 20:27; 23:11; 25:21,23, "And whosoever will be chief among you, *let him be your servant* ... but he that is greatest among you shall be your *servant* ... His lord said unto him, Well done, thou good and faithful *servant*: thou hast been *faithful over a few things*, I will make thee ruler over many things: enter thou into the joy of thy lord."

1 Samuel 13:13; 15:11,17,19,22-23, "And Samuel said to Saul, Thou hast done foolishly: thou hast not kept the commandment of the Lord thy God, which he commanded thee: for now would the Lord have established thy kingdom upon Israel forever ... It repenteth me that I have set up Saul to be king: *for he is turned back from following me, and hath not performed my commandments* ... And Samuel said, *When thou wast little in thine own sight, wast thou not made the head of the tribes of Israel*, and the Lord anointed thee king over Israel? ... Wherefore then *didst thou not obey* the voice of the Lord, but ... didst evil in the sight of the Lord? ... to obey is better than sacrifice, and to hearken than the fat of rams ... *Because thou hast rejected the word of the Lord, he hath also rejected thee from being king.*"

1 Corinthians 4:2, "Moreover it is *required in stewards, that a man be found faithful.*"

Numbers 14:24, "Because Caleb ... hath *followed me fully*, him *will I bring into the land* ... and his seed shall possess it."

Leadership must be balanced if it is to endure. Balanced leadership is a spirit of servanthood that is willing to become assertive for the sake of the larger cause.

In the late 19th century, Friedrich Stiller wrote, "The critical juncture found none but second-rate actors on the political stage, and the decisive moment was neglected because the courageous were deficient in power, and the powerful (were deficient) in sagacity, wisdom, courage and resolution."

In his book, *When Dreams And Heroes Died*, author Arthur Levine tells us what the philosopher Aristotle wrote 2,500 years ago:

> Young men have strong passions ... They would rather do noble deeds than useful ones ... They think they know everything and are always quite sure about it; this, in fact, is why they overdo everything. Old men have lived many years: They often have been taken in ... The result is that they are sure about nothing and under-do everything. They "think" but they never "know." They always add "possibly" or a "perhaps." They guide their lives too much by considerations of what is useful and too little by what is noble ... They lack confidence in the future ... for most things go wrong, or anyway worse than one expects.

Citing the philosopher's words, a commentator on contemporary students wrote, "Like Aristotle's <u>old men</u> – <u>not</u> his young men – today's students live in a time when dreams and heroes have died."

How sad! Young men are often too self-assured and cocky to lead. Old men are too discouraged, pragmatic and opinion-poll conscious to lead. Young men are idealistic. Old men are cynical.

Let us ask the sovereign God to raise up leaders who will be models of servanthood, courage and vision! Leaders who will dare to both dream noble dreams and attempt noble tasks for the glory of God!

Vaclav Havel, President of the Czech Republic, said, "The real test of a man is not when he plays the role that he wants for himself, but when he plays the role destiny has for him." And who rules over our destinies? None but God Himself.

God does something that can actually change the history of a ministry, a city, a state, a nation and, indeed, the world when He puts together **in one human being the unique and compelling combination of servant and visionary! A leader is an obedient servant.** "But he that is greatest among you shall be your servant" (Matthew 23:11).

On hearing of President Truman's relieving General MacArthur of his command in Korea, Dwight Eisenhower said, "When you put on a uniform there are certain inhibitions you accept."

On the one hand, the servant spirit attracts people who are eager to be near that rare quality sometimes called altruism. The man or woman who sincerely wants to meet the needs of others will always be in demand. He or she belongs to an almost extinct breed. Whatever is rare is sought after.

The vision, on the other hand, offers purpose and security to those who cannot "see" the way on their own.

The Greville Diary speaks with great admiration of the Duke of Wellington who embodied both characteristics and captured the attention and loyalty of all of Great Britain. *The Diary* describes Wellington as one who "took more pride in obeying than in commanding." It refers to him as "the humblest of citizens and the most obedient of servants."

Robert Greenleaf said, "In order to be a servant-leader, you must first learn servanthood." Hebrews 5:8 says of Christ, "Though he were a Son, yet learned he obedience by the things which he suffered." Robert E. Lee often signed his letters to Jefferson Davis, President of the Confederacy, in this manner, "I am, with great respect, your obedient servant."

Jim Kennedy wrote, "Train a man and he will become only what you are. Serve and develop a man who is caught up with vision and is dedicated to God, and the sky is the limit."

George VI of England said, "The highest of distinctions is service to others."

Leonardo da Vinci said, "I prefer death to lassitude [listlessness]. I never tire of serving others."

Leo Tolstoy wrote, "The vocation of every man is to serve other people."

Francis Chavasse said, "Praise and service are great healers."

Leadership is remembering that the purest (and most secure) form of leadership is servanthood.

Few followers resent being served. Few followers conspire to "overthrow" a servant. There is nothing to overthrow!

Authoritarian over-lordship generates its own opposition.

Jesus clearly opposed authoritarian over-lordship. Let us note what He said in Matthew 20:25-28:

> But Jesus called them unto him, and said, Ye know that the princes of the Gentiles exercise dominion over them, and they that are great exercise authority upon them.

> But it shall not be so among you: but whosoever will be great among you, let him be your minister;

> And whosoever will be chief among you, let him be your servant:

> Even as the Son of man came not to be ministered unto, but to minister, and to give his life a ransom for many.

Peter, the apostle who did the preaching the day "about three thousand souls" were converted and added to the church, concurred with our Lord in this matter. Peter wrote, "Feed the flock of God which is among you, taking the oversight thereof, not by constraint ... neither as being lords over God's heritage, but being ensamples to the flock" (1 Peter 5:2, 3).

The authoritarian mentality asserts, "You will do it because I say so! You will do it or else!" Psalm 18:35c reads, "Thy gentleness hath made me great." Paul wrote of his ministry in 1 Thessalonians 2:7, "But we were gentle among you, even as a nurse cherisheth her children." He also said, "When I am weak, then am I strong" (2 Corinthians 12:10.)

Dr. Paul Rees said, "If you want a picture of success as heaven measures it, of greatness as God views it, don't look for the blaring of the bands on Broadway; listen, rather, for the tinkle of water splashing into a basin, while God incarnate, in a humility that makes angels hold their breath, sponges the grime from the feet of His undeserving disciples."

After the Gettysburg defeat in 1863, Robert E. Lee sent the following message to Jefferson Davis, President of the Confederacy, "I am as willing to serve now as in the beginning in any capacity and at any post where I can do good. The lower the position, the more suitable to my ability and the more agreeable to my feelings."

Leadership Is ... More Than Management

—⚯—

D. N. Jackson wrote, "The size of a leader is determined by the depth of his convictions, the height of his ambitions, the breadth of his vision and the reach of his love."

I like managers, but many can manage who can not or do not lead. Leadership is more than management. Management may be little more than a perpetuation of the status quo.

William A. Marstele said, "It is important to see the difference between leadership and management. Some institutions are well-managed but poorly led. That is a mating that begets mediocrity." Carl Combs wrote, "An organization can be filled by appointments, but a team must be built by a leader."

When Columbia University asked Eisenhower to consider becoming President of the University, he replied that he thought of himself as a soldier rather than a scholar. Thomas Watson, a trustee of the University replied, "We already have enough scholars ... what we need is a leader of the university."

Management has to do with the implementation of policies, procedures and technicalities. There is certainly a place for the manager. However, **without the creative power of leadership there would be nothing to manage**. Leadership draws people together and sets the direction. Management monitors the quality control of the journey. Both are important. God uses both. But without leadership there is nothing to manage.

While leaders are undeniably called upon from time to time to engage in the nuts and bolts of management (especially when the organization or ministry has a limited staff), ideally a leader is much more of a servant-visionary than he is a manager.

Sheila Murray Bethel says, "Managers have 'to do' lists. Leaders have 'to create' lists."[8]

In John 1:37-41 two of John the Baptist's disciples decide to follow Jesus. They do not follow Jesus because He is a manager. They follow Him because He is a leader. Luke 5:11 tells us that leaders are able to inspire followers to leave "the good life" in hope of a better life, "And when they had brought their ships to land, they [the disciples] forsook all, and followed him [Jesus]."

Napoleon Bonaparte said, "A leader is a dealer in hope."

A leader takes people where they don't necessarily want to go, but ought to be, and leaves them with the feeling that this is where they needed to be all along. The best kind of leadership causes followers to subordinate the *pain* of following to the *joy* of following.

Robert Townsend said, "A leader is a person with a magnet in his heart and a compass in his head."

Leadership Is ... Born

—∿—

It is easy for followers to become enamored with the grandeur of leadership and forget that leadership is a gift from the sovereign God. 1 Corinthians 4:7 says, "And what hast thou that thou didst not receive? Now if thou didst receive it, why dost thou glory, as if thou hadst not received it?" We must also not forget that it is God who likewise sets up unregenerate leaders, by His sovereign permission.

It is the Lord who brings leadership to birth.

And leaders must never forget that God uses followers to give a stewardship of leadership to the leader. There would be no leadership without followship. Scripture is replete with illustrations of how God uses times, circumstances and followship to help create the very leadership that is needed at a given moment in human history.

Leadership is born when a servant-hearted individual obeys God in the opportunity afforded by the crises of his lifetime.

Do you remember what Mordecai asked Esther when she was reluctant to take the lead? "Who knoweth whether thou art come to the kingdom for such a time as this?" (Esther

4:14e) This is the placement or appointment of a man or woman at the right time in the right place.

And listen to Joseph telling his remorseful brothers (followers) how God used them to create his own leadership, "But as for you, ye thought evil against me; but God meant it unto good, to bring to pass, as it is this day, to save much people alive." (Genesis 50:20)

God creates His leaders in specific times and milieux or surroundings.

As he opened his novel, *A Tale Of Two Cities*, Charles Dickens wrote, "It was the best of times; it was the worst of times."

In his essay, "On Leadership" in the introduction to the *World Leaders Past And Present* series, Arthur M. Schlesinger, Jr., writes,

> (Leaders) cannot be effective by themselves. They must act in response to the rhythms of their age. Their genius must be adapted ... "to the recep-tivities of the moment." Leaders are useless without followers. "There goes the mob," said the French politician hearing a clamor in the streets. "I am their leader, (so) I must follow them!"

The balance is that the leader must relate to where the followers are but lift them higher – not follow the poll to the lowest common denominator. Schlesinger continues:

> Great leaders turn the undeveloped emotions of the mob to purposes of their own. They seize on the opportunities of their time, the hopes, fears,

frustrations, crises and potentialities. They succeed when events have prepared the way for them, when the community is awaiting to be aroused, when they can provide the clarifying and organizing ideas. Leadership ignites the circuit between the individual and the mass and thereby alters history.

Leaders are to some degree molded by their followers. No one leads in a vacuum. Followers can, in fact, limit leaders. Followship sets the pattern for leadership.

Matthew 13:58 has this to say about human history's greatest leader, "And He [Jesus] did not many mighty works there because of their unbelief." Whether we like it or not, leaders have to lead in the setting or atmosphere of followship.

Winston Churchill described the birth of leadership with these words, "Real leaders of men do not come forward offering to lead. They show the way, and when it has been found to lead to victory, they accept as a matter of course the allegiance of those who have followed." Churchill's concept reveals, of course, why he was so deeply wounded when the British voters tossed him out of office right after he had led Britain and the entire free world in defeating the Nazis in 1945.

Leadership is born when – and because – God has prepared his man for the critical moment, hour or century. It was God who "found" both Isaiah and Jeremiah (Isaiah 49:5, Jeremiah 1:5).

When a soldier under his command asked Dwight D. Eisenhower to define leadership, the General asked for a piece of string. The soldier returned with the string; Eisenhower laid it on the side of the desk closest to where the soldier was standing. "Now push the string over to me," said Ike. The soldier dutifully took the end of the string between his thumb and index finger and began to try to force it to move across the desk toward the grinning Commander. The string, of course, rebelled and buckled in several places. Eisenhower then took hold of the end of the string closest to him and, with ease, pulled it toward himself.

Leadership Is ... Influence

—🐛—

In *Manfred*, Act 3, Scene 4, Lord Byron describes individuals of influence as "the dead, but sceptred sovereigns, who still rule our spirits from their urns."

Kenneth Blanchard said, "The key to successful leadership ... is influence, NOT AUTHORITY."

Leadership is getting people to help you when they do not have to. Leadership is enlisting the involvement of followship – without coercion.

In the Pensacola Christian College *Update*, Summer 2001, Dr. Arlin Horton, the President and Founder of the college wrote concerning the role of influence:

"The power of influence is reflected in the following questions:

Name the three wealthiest people in the world.

Name four people who have won the Nobel Prize.

Name the last five World Series winners.

How did you do? Most of us do not remember the headliners of yesterday because achievements are eventually forgotten. But try this:

> Name three teachers who influenced you in a school.

> Name four mentors who have taught you a valuable lesson.

> Name five friends who have helped you through difficult times.

The people who truly make a difference in our lives are not the ones with the most credentials."

People want to be led – not driven. People are not cattle!

Great men and women of the past are said to have cast "long shadows" because their lives not only touched those around them, but also reached beyond the grave.

Robert Murray McCheyne said, "Live so as to be missed when you are gone." McCheyne died at the age of 29, and yet the testimony and influence of his godly life still reverberate throughout the Christian church. An American was being shown through St. Peter's Church, Dundee, Scotland. He kept inquiring about the secret of Pastor McCheyne's power. The old sexton, who was showing him around, kept putting the tourist off. Finally they went up a winding staircase into the high pulpit, and then the sexton said to the tourist, "You've been asking after the secret of our Pastor's power. Put your elbows on the pulpit and then put your head in your hands. Now let the tears flow. That's what our Pastor used to do. That was his secret." McCheyne had lived in such a way that he was missed. That is influence.

Each of us needs to ask, "Who am I influencing? What kind of influence am I having?"

How does influence operate?

On one occasion General Dwight D. Eisenhower was asked to explain effective leadership. As the group of men stood around the desk the General asked for a piece of string. He laid the string on the desk. Then he looked at the soldier who had brought the string and said, "Now I want you to take hold of the end of the string closest to you and push it across to me."

As the string was pushed, it buckled and bent and bunched up. The man made little headway and experienced considerable frustration. As soon as it was obvious what was taking place, Eisenhower spoke again and said, "Now let's try something different." With that he took hold of the other end of the string and pulled it across the desk." The string, of course, gave no resistance and willingly followed the pull.

Eisenhower said, "If you pull the string, it will follow you wherever you want it to go. If you try to push it, you meet with nothing but opposition."

He also said, "Leadership is the art of getting someone else to do something you want done because he wants to do it."

The British general, Bernard L. Montgomery, said, "Eisenhower has the power of drawing the hearts of men towards him as a magnet attracts the bits of metal."

Are we pulling people or are we trying to push them?

Machiavelli wrote, "It is not titles that honor men, but men who honor titles."

Sheila Murray Bethel said, "There are people who have no imposing title or formal authority, yet they command [not demand] great personal power. They have an aura about them ... that goes beyond any job description."

Ralph Waldo Emerson said, "Every great institution is the lengthened shadow of a single man." He was talking about influence.

Senator Everett Dirksen said, "The oil can is mightier than the sword." He was referring to leadership by persuasion as opposed to domination by force.

Leadership is influence. Influence reaches where control cannot go.

When Abraham Lincoln was addressing the Springfield Washington Temperance Society in 1842, he made the following remarks: "When the conduct of men is designed to be influenced, persuasion – kind, unassuming persuasion – should be adopted. It is an old and a true maxim that a 'drop of honey catches more flies than a gallon of gall.' So with men ... The heart ... is the great high road to (man's) reason ... If you gain a man's heart, you will find but little trouble in convincing his judgment of the justice of your cause ... On the contrary, assume to dictate to his judgment, or to command his action ... and he will retreat within himself, close all the avenues to his head and his heart; and though your cause be naked truth itself ... you shall no more be able to reach him than to penetrate the hard shell of a tortoise with a rye straw.

"Such is man, and so must he be understood by those who would lead him, even to his own best interest."

Napoleon Bonaparte wrote, "I am much struck with the contrast between Christ's mode of gathering people to himself and the way practiced by Alexander the Great, by Julius Caesar and by myself. The people have been gathered to us by fear. But the people were gathered to Christ by love. Alexander, Caesar and I have been men of war, but Christ was the Prince of Peace. The people have been driven to us; they were drawn to Him. And at this hour millions of men would die for him."

Influence goes way beyond the reach of "control." Influence goes where control cannot go; influence is far more powerful and more lastingly effective than manipulation or intimidation.

The leader who leads by intimidation is characterized by blustery hubris, enemy complexes and self-preserving drivenness.

The leader who leads by influence is secure because he knows that neither life nor death, nor winning or losing, nor success or failure can rob him of the influence of what he is and has been. He demonstrates the poise of one who knows that there is no such thing as an unmitigated failure or an unmitigated triumph. He knows that the seeds of his next achievement lie in his present failure and that every success has its built-in perils.

The manipulator behaves like one who is desperate for the vindication of his existence. The leader has a strong sense of mission which grows out of internalized convictions. He knows that both convictions and influence are immortal.

The one who is content to merely dominate his followers lives in fear because he knows that his control will end with his absence – or death; genuine leadership serves with a confidence that knows even the grave cannot kill influence.

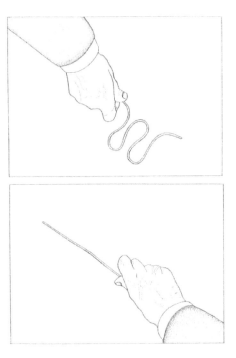

Top: The "push" model of leadership – Authoritarian. This style creates its own rebellion.

Bottom: The "pull" model of leadership – Authoritative. This style draws people to do what they might normally not want to do.

Leadership Is ... Excellence

—〜〜—

Psalm 8:1 reads, "O Lord our Lord, how excellent is thy name in all the earth! who has set thy glory above the heavens."

Psalm 36:7 says, "How excellent is thy lovingkindness, O God! Therefore the children of men put their trust under the shadow of thy wings."

In Philippians 1:10 Paul states his bottom-line prayer request for the believers at Philippi, "That ye may approve things that are excellent; that ye may be sincere and without offence till the day of Christ."

As Christian leaders we must pursue excellence because we serve an excellent God.

The pursuit of excellence is the air that worthy leaders breathe. To be satisfied with the mediocre is to forfeit the right to lead.

Dr. Shelton Smith, the current editor of *The Sword of the Lord*, asked, "Why do we content ourselves with analysis and paralysis? Why do we sit idly at a table with nothing on it and then cry poverty? Why do we poor-mouth? Why doesn't somebody step up to bat and say, 'We're going to knock the ball over the fence'? Why do we content ourselves with bunting instead of trying to hit a home run once in a while?"[10]

In his book, *Incredible Stories Along the Journey*, Dr. James Ray gives us a touching account of the life of Helen Keller. At 19 months of age Helen contracted a disease which left her both blind and deaf. Later she wrote, "Gradually I got used to the silence and darkness that surrounded me and forgot that it had ever been different."

When Helen was seven her parents hired Annie Sullivan from the Perkins Institute for the Blind in Boston. To teach Helen the alphabet, Annie traced the shape of the letters with her fingers on her hand. The pain-staking efforts paid off, and Helen eventually became a world-renown celebrity. She had a personal meeting with every President of the United States from the time she was nine until her death in 1968.

In the author's opinion, the best explanation of the principle of excellence is found in a statement Helen Keller made to the Tennessee Legislature. She said, "When I was young I longed to do great things and could not, so I decided to do small things in a great way."

Aristotle said, "We are what we repeatedly do; excellence then is not an act, but a habit."

The former U.S. Secretary of Education, William Bennett, said, "Most certification today is pure 'credentialism.' It must begin to reflect our demand for excellence, not our appreciation of parchment."

Stonewall Jackson said, "Endeavor to do well everything you undertake."

Ecclesiastes 9:10 reads, "Whatsoever thy hand findeth to do, do it with thy might."

Joubert said, "Mediocrity is excellent to the eye of the mediocre."

In his book, *Excellence*, John W. Gardner writes, "Some people may have greatness thrust upon them. Very few have excellence thrust upon them. They achieve it. They do not achieve it unwittingly, by doin' what comes naturally; and they don't stumble into it in the course of amusing themselves. All excellence involves discipline and tenacity of purpose."

Phillips Brooks wrote, "Sad will be the day for any man when he becomes contented with the thoughts he is thinking and the deeds he is doing – where there is not beating at the doors of his soul some great desire to do something larger which he knows that he was meant and made to do."

Once Benjamin Disraeli scolded the people of England saying, "It is a wretched thing to be gratified with mediocrity when the excellent lies before us."

What are the elements of excellence? Jonathan Edwards said, **"Leadership rises and falls on its view of God."** Our degree of excellence is determined by our view of God. In the opinion of another, "Quality, craftsmanship and tradition are the threads that secure excellence."

Dr. O.P. Gilbert once worried aloud confessing, "As we see it, Baptists are suffering from the frosts of mediocrity. We are too complacent. We are at ease in Zion; and at a time when the channels of communication are glutted with information, our editorials, our sermons, our books and our tracts are mediocre." Dr. Gambrell acknowledged, "We Baptists are many, but not much."

And Phillips Brooks declared, "This fact of the prevalence of mediocrity, or of the average in life, becomes oppressive. It seems to level life into a great, flat, dreary plain. We cannot get rid of ... the demoralization which it brings by simply denying the fact of the preponderance of mediocrity." This is, of course, a perfect description of what takes place under socialism and communism. Brooks once told a Boston audience, "It is time for Boston to get out of the peck and into the bushel."

Dr. Jack Trieber, Pastor of North Valley Baptist Church and President of Golden State Baptist College in Santa Clara, California, wrote, "There is so much mediocrity in this day in which we live. Oftentimes, people seem to be satisfied with the average."

George Eliot, referring to Amos Barton, said, "It is not in his nature to be superlative in anything, unless, indeed, he was superlatively middling, the quintessential (purest) extract of mediocrity."

The Russian writer, Mrs. Andreev, wrote a book with a title that tells it all. Her book is entitled, *Little Men In Great Days*.

A heartbroken pastor once said, "If an automobile had as many useless parts as the average church, it would not run down hill."

When I lived in Columbia, South Carolina, a resident wrote a letter to *The State* newspaper. The editors gave the writer's letter the following caption, "Columbia's Mediocrity

Is Its Best Feature." My inward response was, "Dear Lord, please deliver us from this kind of bland, insipid, timid thinking!"

Joseph Parker, longtime and lionhearted pastor of London's City Temple, lamented, "This world is sick of programs an inch long."

The editorial of the January 27, 1978 issue of *Christianity Today* stated,

> We disapprove of over-stressing the idea of the common man since it is often associated with the unstated notion that everybody in every way should be equal. The dictionary says that the heart of egalitarianism lies in the notion that "all distinctions between groups and individuals (are) inherently unjust." That idea does not agree with life nor with the Bible.

> Robert Louis Stevenson once said, "There are men and classes of men that stand above the common herd." God intended that it should be this way. We are unconvinced by the position of those who believe that distinction is "sui generis" (in and of itself) wrong.

> ... We live in a day when we need more uncommen men, men who are exceptional and outstanding.

We say this not to engender pride – but rather, to provoke to good works, excellent works.

Stradivarius said that he made his violins for eternity. It is reported that not one of the violins of Stradivarius has ever been known to come to pieces or break. Stradivarius never bothered to get a patent on his violins for he knew that no

other violinmaker would be so painstaking in putting superiority into his instruments. Every Stradivarius now in existence is worth several times its weight in gold. Stradivarius
made violins, and then the violins made Stradivarius.

Jonathan Edwards (1703 - 1758)

Jonathan Edwards, a Congregational pastor, was also a brilliant theologian and philosopher. His pulpit power did not
lie in his style. (He read his sermons in a rather unanimated
manner.) It was the content of the messages, quickened by
the moving of the Holy Spirit, that gripped his hearers in
Northampton, Massachusetts. Though mightily used of God
in the colonies' Great Awakening, he was dismissed by the
church when he began to condemn the loose parties in which
the youth of the church were participating. He then served
an American Indian congregation at Stockbridge. In 1757 he
was elected the first president of Princeton University but
died from a smallpox vaccination only a week after taking
the office.

Leadership Is ... Seeing The Invisible

—m—

Proverbs 29:18 says, "Where there is no vision, the people perish." This word "vision" carries the connotation of "revelation." Genuine revelation can only come from God and His Word.

Leaders have to endure. They have to keep hoping when there is no apparent reason to hope. Hebrews 11:27 tells us that Moses, the great catalyst of the Judeo-Christian legal system "endured as seeing Him who is invisible."

Hal Reed said, **"Leadership is the transference of vision."** Stan Toler wrote, **"Vision is the ability to see beyond the obvious." The leader leads in direct proportion to his seeing the invisible.**

Jonathan Swift wrote, "Vision is the art of seeing things invisible."

Helen Keller said, "The most pathetic person in the world is someone who has sight but has no vision."

When Jane and I visited Fort Atkinson, Wisconsin, a few years ago in the fall, we took a walk along the Riverwalk that had been so carefully engineered and constructed. Quite unexpectedly and suddenly we came upon a mounted plaque. The plaque read, "The engineering is secondary to the vision." The statement was attributed to Al Haukom.

One of the saddest moments of my life was one particular moment when I stood with a dear friend who had tried to plant a church and not succeeded. We were standing looking out a large window at a piece of property the church I was pastoring had just purchased. My friend asked, "So what are you going to do with that new land?"

I described what I had in mind in some detail.

Finally he spoke, and there was a note of wistful regret in his voice. He said, "You can really see that over there, can't you?" Then he paused and added, "I never could see things like that." I wanted to weep.

Dr. Elmer Towns said, "The ten largest churches in North America were large in their pastors' hearts long before they were large on the street corner." (This is not to emphasize the importance of largeness but to underscore the need for vision.)

Frank Gaines wrote, "Only he who can see the invisible can do the impossible."

Napoleon Bonaparte said, "The world is run by imagination."

Thomas Sowell said, "Visions are the silent shapers of our thought."

A couple I know who were looking for property for the church they had started in Tennessee were looking at a rundown building formerly used as a meeting place for another group. The carpet was lime green; the ceiling was leaky; there were stains on the carpet. The wife wept. (That was understandable.) The husband said, "This has real possibilities. We could put the platform over there and the ...." He had vision!

John Ruskin said, "The greatest thing a human soul ever does in this world is to see something and tell what it saw in a plain way. Hundreds of people can talk for one who can think, but thousands can think for one who can see. To see clearly is poetry, prophecy and religion, all in one."

Haddon Robinson wrote, "You are given a situation. What you are [character] determines what you see [vision]; what you see determines what you do [action]."

Another said, "The person who cannot see the ultimate becomes a slave to the immediate." And still another wrote, "Make no small plans for they have no power to stir your soul."

Sam Foss, the 19th century poet of the Far West left us this piece of inspiration.

Bring me men to match my mountains,
Bring me men to match my plains,
Men with empires in their purpose
And new eras in their brains.

The following quote is attributed both to George Bernard Shaw and Robert Frost, "You see things, and you say, 'Why?' But I dream things that never were, and I say, 'Why not?'"

To seize opportunities you have to first *see* opportunities.

In concluding our look at seeing the invisible let us note three important principles relating to the development and growth of it.

1. The vision of a Christian needs to be for others. Bob Carroll writes, "Napoleon was excessively focused on his own career at the expense of any great interest in his fellow humans. Had his vision been wider, he might be remembered not only as a great hero, but also as a great man."

2. The vision of a leader is often born out of agony and pain. Alexander Solzhenitsyn said, "A hard (or difficult) life sharpens the vision." Beecher wrote, "Tears are often the telescope through which men see far into heaven."

3. The vision must be regularly rehearsed to the followers. Ezra Earl Jones wrote, "Leaders have to state the vision and keep it before the people. They must also often remind the followers of the progress that is being made to achieve the vision. Otherwise, followers may assume they are failing and give up."

Leadership Is ... Purpose

—ᴍ—

In Philippians 3:14 the apostle Paul writes, "I press toward the mark for the prize of the high calling in God in Christ Jesus."

Pertocci said, "No man knows what he is living for until he knows what he'll die for." We get courage by getting a higher purpose, by becoming dispensable in a cause bigger than ourselves.

When Latimer and Ridley were about to be burned at the stake, the elder noticed the faintest, slightest look of fear and reservation cross the younger man's face. So he said, "Never mind. Today we light a fire that will be seen around the world." And it was ... and still is.

John Wesley said, "All our people die well."

The Bible says, "They overcame him by the blood of the Lamb, and by the word of their testimony, and they loved not their lives unto the death" (Revelation 12:11). **Nothing ennobles a leader like a sense of higher purpose; there is no substitute for it.**

When Stonewall Jackson and his bride Ellie visited the Plains of Abraham where General Wolfe died defeating General Montcalm, Jackson swept his arms wide and uttered the words which Wolfe had declared when he was dying, "I die content!" Then Jackson added, "To die as he died, who would not die content?!"

One of the most profound lessons I have ever learned is this: to become dispensable in a cause bigger than yourself is to lose all fear of man and what the developments of time can do to you.

G.K. Chesterton said, "Courage means a strong desire to live taking the form of a readiness to die."

Archibald Rutledge once wrote a delightful little book entitled, *My Colonel And His Lady*. In his book he tells an interesting experience which he had as a lad on the Santee River in central South Carolina. This particular occasion had to do with an old African-American river boat captain who piloted the ferry boat "Foam." The boat was dirty, odorous and badly kept. But one day when Dr. Rutledge went down to the river, he found the "Foam" completely transformed. It was clean from stem to stern. It fairly gleamed and glistened in the sunlight. The boat's brass had been polished until it shone like so many mirrors. The bilge water had gone from behind the seats, and the deck had been scoured to the raw wood. No less miraculous was the transformation in the African-American captain himself. He was shining and immaculate. His face beamed; his eyes sparked; he sat behind the "Foam's" wheel with an open Bible on his lap. When Dr. Rutledge asked him the reason for this wonderful change, he said, "I got a glory!"

Some great ideas had gotten into the captain's thinking, and some great aspirations had gotten into his blood stream. These had made him a different man.

He now had the glory of a lighted mind, the glory of a quickened personality. He had the glory of a great ambition. Spiritual truth and reality had touched him in exactly the right places. The transformation so apparent in the river boat was only a manifestation of a more important transformation in the captain himself. His work itself had not changed; he was still a river boat captain. But now he was the best river boat captain on the Santee. Henceforth, whatever he did would indicate his own change of life, and his life's work would indicate his life's glory.

The story of the river boat captain is the story of every man, for every man manifests his greatness in his work. If he isn't great in what he does, he isn't great. No man can have a high and noble character while engaged in petty or unworthy employment, for whatever the pursuits of men are, their characters will be similar.

You can't have a glory while you have bilge water under your seats or a sour attitude about life and the price it is exacting from you.

The leader gets "a glory" when he loses himself in a purpose higher than himself. This is what ennobles him and puts the glow on his face that attracts followers.

Winston Churchill (1874 - 1965)

Though neglected by his socialite mother, Jenny, and virtually spurned by his aloof and unfeeling father, this short,
red-headed Brit became the hero of the free world. Lord
Randolph shipped the boy off to Harrow School and there-
after consistently treated him as an inconvenience to his own
political career. The great disappointments of this rejection
probably, in fact, burned a steel into Churchill that prepared
him for the lonely pressures he would face when he publicly
disagreed with the appeasement policies of Prime Minister
Neville Chamberlain and sounded the trumpet of alarm
regarding Adolph Hitler. He became Prime Minister of Great
Britain in 1940 and served until he was ungratefully dumped
by the British people in 1945. Wilderness years followed,
but his people came to their senses and reelected him in
1951. He overcame an early speech impediment to become a
magnificent orator. When Sir Winston died, the world cried.

Leadership Is ... Woundedness

—⟋⟍—

In his commentary on *The Life of David*, Arthur Pink quotes an unnamed author and relates the quote to David's second sojourn with Achish when, because King Saul was seeking to kill him, David left the land of Israel and went to live in the land of the Philistines (1 Samuel 27). In a comment on this, the unnamed author states, "It is in one sense, a very easy matter to get out of the place of trial; but then we get out of the place of blessing also."

Psalm 119:71 says, "It is good for me that I have been afflicted; that I might learn thy statutes."

Plato said, "All learning has an emotional base."

The story of many a leader is the story of the oyster and the pearl. These leaders create out of irritation, difficulty and suffering. Their creativity is born out of hurt.

Jesus did not liken the kingdom of God to a diamond, but to a pearl. Of all precious stones, the pearl has the humblest origin. It begins with a wound and is created out of God's resources for healing the wound.

Robert Bly said, "Where a man's wound is, that is where his genius (effectiveness) will be. That is exactly where he will give his major gift to the community."

King David was sensitized by the pain of the jealousy and rejection of his brothers and by being the object of Saul's murderous rages.

Joseph experienced the pain of jealousy and rejection also at the hand of his brothers. He was cast away and sold while he was very young.

Dr. Pierre Rentchnick's research sheds some amazing light on the inter-relationship of woundedness, creativity and leadership. He had been studying how disease affected political leaders. When he read the life stories of leaders who had a great influence on world history, he was struck by the astonishing coincidence that so many of them had been orphans. Some had lost parents in infancy; some had lost theirs later through separation; others had simply been abandoned. Rentchnick compiled a list of almost 300 of the most influential names in history, including Alexander the Great, Julius Caesar, George Washington, Napoleon, Golda Meir, Adolf Hitler and Fidel Castro.

He published his findings in a book with the striking title, *Do Orphans Lead The World?* He concluded that what many would consider emotional deprivation may arouse an exceptional willpower which can be turned to either good or evil.

Intrigued by Rentchnick's discovery, Paul Tournier, who was himself an orphan, took up the study. Soon he realized that many of the most influential religious leaders were also virtual orphans. For example, Moses' parents had to give him up because of the persecution of the Hebrews in Egypt, and he became the son of the princess. Joseph was virtually orphaned as a young man. Muhammad's parents died before he was one year old. Confucius lost his father at the age of one. Pascal lost his mother at three.

Tournier extended his research to include leaders who have suffered other deprivations, and his conclusions suggested a close link between the experience of deprivation and creativity. For the leader, creativity is essential. Life is constantly changing but people always fear change. Not all change is good. Unscriptural change should be resisted. However, the Christian leader is responsible to help followers adapt to biblically justifiable change. Leaders must be creative or become obsolete.

Suffering or deprivation may feed the springs of leadership by increasing creativity. Indeed, the Bible states this very principle in 2 Timothy 2:12, "If we suffer, we shall also reign with him."

And this is exactly what George Matheson said in his classic hymn, "O Love That Wilt Not Let Me Go."

"I trace the rainbow through the rain ...
I lay in dust life's glory dead,
And from the ground there blossoms red
Life that shall endless be."

As a young man, in *The River War*, Winston Churchill wrote out of the painful experience of being neglected and ignored by his father, Lord Randolph Churchill. He said, "A boy deprived of his father's care often develops, if he escapes the perils of youth, an independence of vigor and thought which may restore in after life the heavy loss of early days."

Thirty-five years later, when a great man of affairs, Churchill added that "famous men are usually the product of an unhappy childhood. The stern compression of circumstances, the spur of slights and taunts in early years, are needed to evoke that ruthless fixity of purpose and tenacious motherwit without which great actions are seldom accomplished."

The difficulty which the great missionary Paul referred to as "a thorn in the flesh" (2 Corinthians 12:7) *makes* the missionary, the statesman and the soldier alike. As Psalm 119:71 says, "It is good for me that I have been afflicted."

A. W. Tozer said, "It is doubtful whether God can greatly use a man until He has deeply wounded him."

Moses said that he could not speak. Churchill also had a speech impediment in early life. Students at Brienne-le-Chateau military school made fun of Napoleon's small stature and his Corsican accent.

Do we dare speculate on the reason for the connection between woundedness and leadership? We do for we do not think the connection is hard to see.

The wounding process (or the pain) keenly sensitizes. One cannot lead effectively without possessing sensitivity to needs, opportunities, possible courses of action and consequences. Sensitivity may well be the sixth sense of every effective leader.

Insensitivity, displayed in the incidents referred to earlier, spoiled the prospects of General George Patton's career.

Aristotle said that we cannot learn apart from pain.

Eleanor Doan observed, "The school of affliction graduates rare scholars."

Aeschylus (525-456 B.C.) said, "Wisdom comes by suffering."

William Wordsworth said, "Wisdom is oftentime nearer when we stoop than when we soar."

Alan E. Nelson wrote, "Broken leaders produce whole followers."

The blind Baptist poet, John Milton, wrote,

Is it true, O Christ in heaven, that the highest suffer the most?
That the mark of rank in nature is capacity for pain?
That the anguish of the singer makes the sweetness of the strain?

A British author said, "Pain is this grave but kindly teacher of immortal secrets, this conferrer of liberty."

Golda Meir said, "Those who do not know how to weep with their whole heart don't know how to laugh either."

Dana Greene wrote, "Borderland experiences (periods of doubt, difficulty and pain) may produce despair and blackness but will probably also offer the opportunity for enormous creativity."

Thomas á Kempis remarked, "When looking for a leader ... we inquire how skillful he is ... We should be inquiring how poor in spirit ... and meek he is."

Alan E. Nelson also said, "If you are a pastor or other Christian leader, look for lay leaders and staff who have been broken in the right place. No amount of talent, charisma, or experience will make up for an unbroken associate."

E. H. Chapin said, "Out of suffering have emerged the strongest souls; the most massive characters are seared with scars."

Alexis Carrel wrote, "Man cannot remake himself without suffering, for he is both the marble and the sculptor."

Edward Johnson said, "Success and suffering are vitally and organically linked. If you succeed without suffering, it is because someone else has suffered before you; if you suffer without succeeding, it is that someone else may succeed after you."

J. L. Allen wrote, "It's the defeat more than anything else that hurts you! Defeat is always the hardest thing for you to stand, even in trifles. But don't you know that we have to be defeated in order to succeed? Most of us spend half our lives fighting for things that would only destroy us if we got them. A man who has never been defeated is usually a man who has been ruined."

An unknown poet wrote,

When God wants to drill a man
And thrill a man
And skill a man,
When God wants to mold a man
To play the noblest part;
When He yearns with all His heart
To create so great and bold a man
That all the world shall be amazed,
Watch His methods, watch His ways!
How He ruthlessly perfects
Whom He royally elects!
How He hammers him and hurts him,
And with mighty blows converts him
Into trial shapes of clay which
Only God understands;
While his tortured heart is crying
And he lifts beseeching hands!
How He bends but never breaks
When his good He undertakes;
How He uses whom He chooses
And with every purpose fuses him;
By every act induces him
To try His splendor out –
God knows what He's about.

In the May 10, 1996 editorial in the Hammond, Indiana, *Times*, to which I referred briefly in an earlier chapter, George Will wrote,

> The work of the last 13 years of Franklin Delano Roosevelt's life cannot properly be contemplated without reference to the affliction that left him a paraplegic for the last 24 years of his life. He probably would not have become president, and certainly would not have become the long-headed and tough

president he was, without passing through the furnace of polio ... The disease catalyzed the transformation of the debonair young swell, skating along on charm and connections, into the brilliant and broadly empathetic politician ... the temperament FDR exhibited in the 1930s and 1940s was forged in the 1920s. The iron entered into his soul when he performed with heroic ebullience the excruciating exercises necessary to make his legs ready for steel braces.

It is as FDR's biographer, Geoffrey Ward, says, "If you want to learn the secret of a man's success, you must look at what made him before the trumpet blast turned the attention of the world upon him. It was pain that made FDR."

Booker T. Washington created the Tuskegee Institute, an acclaimed school for African Americans, out of a stable and a henhouse on an abandoned farm near Tuskegee, Alabama. He wrote, "Success is to be measured not so much by the position that one has reached in life as by the obstacles which he has overcome while trying to succeed."

Booker T. Washington (1856 - 1915)

Born a slave in Hales Ford, Virginia, Washington became a teacher in 1879. In 1881 the town of Tuskegee, Alabama, was looking for a principal for a new free school for blacks. General Armstrong recommended the brilliant Booker, who was only 25 years old. The first classes were held in a shack. Soon he borrowed $200 to make a down payment on a dilapidated farm outside of town. Within a few years the school was famous all across the country. Booker insisted the students be well dressed for class. He would not approve of today's blue jeans and T-shirts. The acclaimed educator said, "I am determined to permit no man to narrow or degrade my soul by making me hate him."

Leadership Is … The Right Use Of Power

—ɯ—

1 Peter 5:2 gives inspired advice to those leaders who are elder-pastors. "Feed the flock of God which is among you, taking the oversight thereof, not by constraint, but willingly; not for filthy lucre, but of a ready mind. Neither as being lords over God's heritage, but being ensamples to the flock."

And the same spirit will apply in the life and conduct of a wise leader in any other field.

General Dwight Eisenhower said, "You do not lead by hitting people over the head – that's assault, not leadership."

I read an amazing story in the June 23, 1996, *Orlando Sentinel*. A crowd of anti-Ku Klux Klan demonstrators had attacked a man at a pro-Klan rally. The pro-Klan man had been knocked to the street. The anti-Klan people were beating him up. Eighteen-year-old African-American Keshia Thomas draped her body over the pro-Klan man on the street and said, "Just because you beat somebody doesn't mean you are going to change his mind."

What a wise young lady! What a leader! She understood that you do not lastingly change people or history by brute force. You change people by the power of influence from the inside out!

Pittacus said, **"The measure of a man is what he does with power."**

Oswald Sanders wrote, "Paul, like his Master ... did not try to exert a cultic control over the minds of his followers ... His ultimate reliance was on the promised cooperation of the Holy Spirit."

Abraham Lincoln echoed the sentiments of Pittacus and said, "Nearly all men can stand adversity, but if you want to test a man's character, give him power."

Henry Ward Beecher wrote, "Greatness lies not in being strong, but in the right use of strength."

Sheila Murray Bethel said, "The higher up you go, the more gently you reach down."

Thomas Connelly wrote, "Robert E. Lee's courtesy to junior officers and private soldiers reflected his great human spirit ... He was a gentleman and saw no need to prove it."

Lee himself said, "Forbearing the use of power is not only a touchstone ... The manner in which an individual enjoys certain advantages over others is the test of a true gentleman. The power which the strong have over the weak (should not) show needlessly."

True power does not have to flaunt itself.

Lee's credo was, "A gentleman possesses authority, knows it, and applies it judiciously. He does not needlessly and unnecessarily remind an offender of a wrong ... He does not make a practice of publicly humiliating his subordinates. One of the strongest rebukes Lee ever gave to General J.E.B. Stuart (who was extremely late for a preplanned rendezvous and had gravely jeopardized the outcome of the battle) was, "General Stuart, where have you been?"

Becky Brodin said, "Leadership is not wielding authority – it is empowering people."

McAlindon wrote, "We can no longer distinguish leaders from mere power holders. The real leader directs as though he had no authority. He leads on the basis of the quality of his mind, his ideas, his concerns, his values and his life ... He is not afraid to truly love."

John Wallace wrote, "There's an old saying, 'Power corrupts.' Yes, but power also purifies; Jesus used it so. Power deprives, but power also provides. Power destroys, but power also constructs. Power is necessary to accomplish anything. It is the use of power that determines its character."[11]

Leadership is preserved when the leader is not impressed by his own power but, rather, remembers to give God the glory for any accomplishments.

Leadership Is ... Weaker When It Is Authoritarian

—ɱ—

"For Saul had (said), Cursed be the man that eateth any food until evening, that I may be avenged on mine enemies. So none of the people tasted any food" (I Samuel 14:24, 29).

In the authoritarian system of leadership insecurity overcompensates. The authoritarian leader is the "bravado" type. This leader's attitude and behavior demonstrate distrust, lack of concern, lack of responsiveness, disrespect, lack of acceptance, lack of support and disapproval of followers. King Saul and General George Patton were authoritarian leaders.

The results of authoritarian leadership include:

1. Defensiveness and concern for personal security, protection, power and status. This, in turn, results in self-centeredness and an inability to admit weaknesses or mistakes.

2. Lack of confidence. This leads to caution, inflexibility and inability to relinquish the old and explore the new.

3.   Feelings of anger, resentment, hate, hostility, aggression, bewilderment, frustration, dissatisfaction, disappointment, grief and withdrawal.

4.   Mutual, reciprocal fear and distrust.

5.   Conflict and competition.

6.   Avoidance of confrontation, openness or revealing of differences.

7.   Use of power over others; dictatorial and arbitrary decision making.

8.   Deception, dishonesty, lack of integrity, incongruence and lack of responsibility.

9.   Negativism, pessimism, cynicism.

10.   Attitudes and behavior of distrust, lack of concern and lack of responsiveness toward the leader and other followers.

11.   Preoccupation with fixing blame instead of channeling energy into fixing the problem.

                    - adapted from *Success* magazine, July, 1981

Leadership Is ... Stronger When It Is Authoritative

—ɯ—

"(Now the man Moses was very meek, above all the men which were upon the face of the earth)" (Numbers 12:3).

In the authoritative system of leadership, strength walks meekly. Moses, Jesus, the apostle Paul and General Dwight Eisenhower led authoritatively. The leader's attitude and behavior demonstrate trust, concern, responsiveness, respect, support and encouragement of followers.

The results of authoritative leadership include:

1. Freedom from defensiveness and concern for power, status or security. This allows a follower to be self-lessly task-oriented and to admit mistakes.

2. Confidence. This allows one to be more flexible and objective, to entertain new ideas and to abandon the irrelevant.

3. Warm feelings toward others, appreciation, satisfaction, cooperation and involvement.

4. Mutual, reciprocal, growth-producing relationships.

5. Harmony and team spirit.

6. Willingness to engage in confrontation and interplay of differences without fear of personal conflict.

7. Shared power, participative decision making and problem solving.

8. Honesty, integrity, congruence and responsibility.

9. Positivism, optimism.

10. Attitudes and behavior of trust, concern and responsiveness toward the leader and other followers.

-adapted from *Success* magazine, July, 1981.

G. Beauchamp Vick (1901- 1975)

George Beauchamp Vick was born in Russellville, Kentucky. He completed the four years of military cadet training in three. After serving as the superintendent of three Sunday School departments at the First Baptist Church of Fort Worth, Texas, Dr. Vick served as the music associate of evangelists Wade House and Mordecai Ham from 1930 – 1935. In 1936 he assumed responsibility for the Temple Baptist Church in Detroit, Michigan. In 1950 he became President of the Baptist Bible College of Springfield, Missouri. He served both ministries simultaneously until his death in 1975. In the 39 years of his leadership in Detroit, the church saw 50,101 additions.

Leadership Is ... Involvement
With Followship

—◦〜◦—

In John 1: 14, 17, 18, the Bible says, "And the Word was made flesh, and dwelt among us, (and we beheld his glory, the glory as of the only begotten of the Father,) full of grace and truth ... For the law was given by Moses, but grace and truth came by Jesus Christ ... No man hath seen God at any time; the only begotten Son, which is in the bosom of the Father, he hath declared him."

Leadership is "in the field," "hands on" involvement in the lives of followship.

Leaders have to "meddle" and get their hands dirty. A leader cannot afford to have his head in the clouds or "live above the fray."

The one who wants that luxury forfeits leadership. He puts himself out of the loop of what is happening and has no one to blame but himself. Detached leadership places both itself and its followers in peril.

He who spends too much time in his ivory tower soon forfeits his leadership. The only way to really know what is going on down on the ground is to spend time there yourself

– on a regular basis. **Detached leadership places both itself and its followers in peril.**

Mark 3:14 tells us that when the Lord Jesus chose His disciples "He ordained twelve, that they should be *with Him*." Leadership cannot lead without regularly associating with followship.

Dr. G. Beauchamp Vick, longtime pastor of Temple Baptist Church, Detroit, Michigan, simultaneously served as president of Baptist Bible College in Springfield, Missouri. Often, when the subject of leadership came up, Dr. Vick would say, "This thing is more caught than taught."

The leader learns *how* he is going to get followers where they need to be by listening to them. In order to hear followers talking the leader must spend time "at the front" with them.

Former Secretary of State Dean Rusk said, "The best way to persuade is with your ears."

Sheila Murray Bethel wrote, "Listening is more than half of communicating."

The leader who loves his followers enough to listen to them is going a long way toward cementing their loyalty to him. He knows that listening to others in a sympathetic and understanding manner is a major part of getting along with people.

One of the elements of personal charisma is the art of listening intently. Oliver Wendell Holmes said, "Too few people practice the 'white magic' of being good listeners."

Writing of Napoleon Bonaparte, D. E. Hoste said, "He was a good listener and possessed in a high degree the gift of applying the special knowledge of others to a particular set of circumstances."

Leadership Is ...
Having A Sense Of Humor
That Defuses Tension

—ɰ—

General Fox Conner said to General Eisenhower, "Always take your job seriously; never yourself."

He who takes himself too seriously may be on his way to becoming proud. There has only been One who had the right and reason to have a Messianic complex, and that is the Messiah, Jesus Christ.

Humor abounds in the halls of influence. Merle Miller reports that an acquaintance of Douglas MacArthur said, "If Caesar didn't look like MacArthur, he should have."

Wise men take a lesson from former President Ronald Reagan. They make themselves the butt of humor. They never make a joke at the expense of another person or race.

"A word fitly spoken is like apples of gold in pictures of silver" (Proverbs 25:11.)

It is amazing how a leader simply and off-handedly pointing out one of his own foibles can break the ice that has gathered over the pond of a difficult speech or board meeting.

Let the leader take care that in his own eyes he has not become the cause. The cause is still ... the cause. Remember that the cause has to survive and thrive, but we do not. We are not God's answer to or for everything.

The leader who is always morose and down may have begun to believe that the cause is having a bad day every time *he* is having a bad day! This kind of self-importance is counter-productive and unbecoming to a leader. It reveals self-love and self-pity.

The leader who is always sad needs some fresh air and some recreation.

Leadership Is ...
Exercising The Courage
Of Your Convictions

—ɯ—

ourage is not the absence of fear. It is persevering in the path of your convictions in spite of your fear.

In Acts 4 we read of the time when the religious authorities, fearing the growing popularity of the Christians – especially after the healing of a lame man, called Peter and John in and commanded them not to speak or teach in the name of Jesus. Peter and John answered, "Whether it be right in the sight of God to hearken unto you more than unto God, judge ye. For we cannot but speak the things which we have seen and heard" (verses 19-20). Peter and John were released, went to a gathering of fellow believers, and had a prayer meeting. The Bible tells us (verse 29) part of their prayer, "And now, Lord, behold their threatenings: and grant unto thy servants, that with all boldness they may speak thy word." Verse 31 says, "And they spake the word of God with boldness." However, had they not had some temptation to fear, it would not have been necessary to pray for boldness.

The late Senator Barry Goldwater said, "Timidity encourages conflict; courage prevents it."

King David was a highly successful military leader. He wrote, "What time I am afraid, I will trust in thee" (Psalm 56:3). The next verse records his resolve that he would not long remain intimidated by man, "In God I will praise his word, in God I have put my trust, I will not fear what flesh can do unto me."

David was motivated by his trust and confidence in God. He was also motivated by convictions which had been born out of his love for truth. David said, "Therefore I hate every false way" (Psalm 119:104).

It is impossible to really lead without convictions. You may hold an office or have a title but you will just be putting in time and drawing a paycheck if you do not have a core set of convictions that pull you on.

James Black said, "Borrowed beliefs have no power." Belief fuels passion, and passion rarely fails.

Dr. Bob Jones, Sr., said, "Every successful man I have ever met had come at some time under the dominating power of a great truth."

Theodore Roosevelt said, "It is a wicked thing to be neutral between right and wrong."

Walter Lippmann said, "The final test of a leader is that he leaves behind in other people the convictions and the will to carry on."

A conviction is a fire in the belly.

Alexander F. Laidlaw, a Canadian outstanding in adult education, identifies two characteristics that all leaders have in common:

1. They are deeply attached to an idea or a set of ideas. Great leaders are men of strong convictions. They believe in something very deeply. We may not admire what they stand for, but there can never be any doubt that they have firm beliefs. So, leadership starts in the mind of the leader – it has its foundation in ideas and a philosophy. Leaders are devoted to a cause.

2. The leader is able in one way or another to transmit his ideas and convictions to others, and in such a way as to make others follow him. And ideas can be communicated in other ways besides speech – some leaders get their ideas across by the written word, by books.

Robert E. Speer wrote, "The heart has reasons that reason does not know. It is the heart that feels God, not the reason. There are truths that are felt and truths that are proved, for we know the truth not only by reason but by the intuitive conviction which may be called the heart. The primary truths are not demonstrable and yet our knowledge of them is nonetheless certain ... Truth may be above reason and yet not contrary to reason."

John Bowers, biographer of Stonewall Jackson, said, "Often a man does not know what is deepest in his heart until his will is tested." J. Oswald Sanders wrote, "Opinions cost us only breath, but convictions often cost life itself."[12]

The heart has its reasons. We may not realize what we love until we seem about to lose it.

A leader can only galvanize and motivate his followers at the point of his convictions. The greater the conviction, the stronger the leader. Only convictions leave lasting impressions. Impressions influence. Influence is, as we have seen ... leadership! Strong convictions engender strong allegiance.

In *The Glory of the Ministry*, the celebrated Greek scholar, A.T. Robertson, wrote, "It is not a preacher's wisdom but his conviction which imparts itself to others. Real flame kindles another flame. Men with convictions will speak and will be heard ... No amount of reading or intellectual brilliance will take the place of thorough conviction and sincerity."

In 1953, after being sworn in as President at the U.S. Capitol, Dwight Eisenhower prayed, "Give us, we pray, the power to discern clearly right from wrong, and allow all our words and actions to be governed thereby."

Leaders are expected to be opinion framers – not poll takers. The taking of polls has helped to produce a generation of barometers when what we need is a generation of leaders who have convictions.

General Douglas MacArthur paraphrased another writer and said, "People grow old only by deserting their ideals. Years may wrinkle the skin, but to give up interest wrinkles the soul ... When ... your heart is covered with the snows of pessimism and the ice of cynicism, then and only then are you grown old."

In her book *Fearless Speaking*, Lilyan Wilder encouraged all public speakers to communicate transparently out of their convictions. She wrote, "Speak from the core of what is meaningful to you, and find acceptance or rejection of your beliefs. Experience the strength that comes from that acceptance or rejection."

Theodore ("Teddy") Roosevelt (1858 - 1919)

Young "Teedie" was filled with energy, curiosity and determination. Through rigid exercise he overcame childhood asthma and built up unusual physical strength. He graduated from Harvard in 1880. When 23 he won election to the New York State Assembly. Both his wife Alice and his mother died on February 14, 1884. In sorrow he left politics and became a rancher in the Dakota Territory. He became the youngest man to ever assume the Presidency when William McKinley was assassinated in 1901. He liked to take family members and friends out to look at the stars. After a time he would say, "I suppose we are all small enough now. Let's go in and go to bed."

Leadership Is ... Self-Discipline

—⚏—

Proverbs 25:28 says, "He that hath no rule over his own spirit is like a city that is broken down, and without walls." Lack of self-discipline leaves a man vulnerable. His flanks are unprotected.

The Roman Empire collapsed because she had a succession of leaders who could not control their own appetites.

J. Oswald Sanders wrote, "A leader is able to lead others because he disciplines himself." The undisciplined man will not lead for very long. He will be defeated through over-indulgence of physical appetites or laziness.

Dwight Eisenhower said, "When you put on a uniform, there are certain inhibitions you accept." We are living in a decadent society as evidenced by the wholesale and widespread casting off of inhibitions. We are living in a largely leaderless, do-your-own-thing, let-it-all-hang-out, if-it-feels-good-do-it generation. It is no coincidence that the most uninhibited generation of the last millennium is also the most leaderless generation of the last millennium.

Robert Thornton Henderson said, "Most of the significant things done in the world were done by persons who were either too busy or too sick! There are few ideal and leisurely settings for the disciplines of growth."

General George Patton declared, "You cannot be disciplined in great things and undisciplined in small things."

In a letter to his children, Robert E. Lee wrote, "At times the temptation to relax will be hard upon you, but will grow feebler and more feeble by constant resistance ... I know it will confirm you in your present resolve to try and do your best ... Hold yourself above every mean action. Be strictly honorable in every act, and be not ashamed to do right."

Leadership Is ... The Faculty
Of Clear Decision

—m—

The Bible records the response of Peter and Andrew, and later of James and John, when Jesus called them to follow Him, "And they straightway left their nets, and followed him ... And they immediately left the ship and their father, and followed him" (Matthew 4:20, 22). In Acts 16:10, we read of a moment when Paul made a decision, "And after he had seen the vision, immediately we endeavored to go into Macedonia, assuredly gathering that the Lord had called us for to preach the gospel unto them."

The leader must learn to separate the decisive from the secondary. Nothing can happen without a decision. If you want things to happen, you must make decisions.

Field Marshall Montgomery said, "A leader must have the power of clear decision."

Brigadier-General Basil Duke described Stonewall Jackson as follows: "His capacity for prompt decision and adherence to the judgments he formed was very remarkable."

Wilfred A. Peterson said, "Decision is the spark that ignites action."[13]

H. A. Hopf wrote, "Indecision is debilitating, it feeds upon itself; it is, one might almost say, habit-forming. Not only that, but it is contagious; it transmits itself to others."

President Andrew Jackson said, "Take time to deliberate, but when the time for action arrives, stop thinking and go in."

The leader must not pause to regroup when there is opportunity lying in his front.

Julius Caesar made one of history's most famous decisions in 49 B.C. His decision is so famous that the location it involved has passed down into our phraseology as a word picture that describes a decision that takes one past the point of no return.

Do you know what that decision was? Probably you do.

In 49 B.C. Julius Caesar crossed the Rubicon River launching a military invasion of Rome and initiating the Roman Civil War. Caesar had finally given up on negotiations aimed at ending his dispute with Pompey.

In so doing, he was committing treason, violating Sulla's law prohibiting a provincial governor from commanding troops outside his dominion. Caesar realized he was taking an irreversible step. As his troops marched into Italy, he uttered the immortal phrase, "The die ... is cast."

The expression "crossing the Rubicon" is used today in many languages. To "cross the Rubicon" is to make a decision that cannot be reversed.[14]

Leadership Is ... Risk Taking

—ɷ—

A cts 15:26 describes Paul and Barnabas as "men that have hazarded their lives for the name of our Lord Jesus Christ." Acts 20:24 records Paul saying, "But none of these things move me, neither count I my life dear unto myself, so that I might finish my course ... " And, at another time, Paul wrote, "Yea doubtless, and I count all things but loss for the excellency of the knowledge of Christ Jesus my Lord: for whom I have suffered the loss of all things, and do count them but dung, that I may win Christ" (Philippians 3:8).

As the details of the future are never a guaranteed thing, the leader must be prepared to take those leaps of faith that others call "risks." He who wants to deal only in the commerce of sure things will never make a leader. He won't even make a good follower.

C.S. Lewis said, "The only people who achieve much are those who want knowledge so badly that they seek it while the conditions are still unfavorable. **Favorable conditions never come.**"

Someone else said, "Progress in life is not measured by security but by growth; and growth means taking occasional risks." Fifty people over 95 years of age were asked to name three things they would do differently if they could live their life over. One of the most popular answers which came up again and again was, "I would take more risks."

Nothing ventured, nothing gained!

Colonel Joseph Ives said, "If there is one man in either army, Confederate or Federal, head and shoulders above every other in audacity, it is General Robert E. Lee. His name might be audacity. He will take more desperate chances and take them quicker than any other general in this country."

Taking a risk is often the only way to learn what works and what doesn't. Every inventor is a risk-taker. We have the electric light bulb today because Thomas Edison took hundreds of risks.

General John E. Long of the U.S. Army said,

Risk taking … is part of my profession. It's an inescapable fact that leaders must be able to determine the best course of action for each situation. Sometimes that means breaking rules or flying in the face of an accepted way of doing things. The leader says, "It's the right thing to do, even if it doesn't fit the model. We will take the risk. We will take any consequences. We believe that if we do it well, our superiors and subordinates will accept that it was the right thing to do."

Every organization needs risk takers. Taking risks relieves tension and stress. Then you can go out and get things done, and that, in turn, lessens risks. I don't mean that you shouldn't have sound advice or

make joint decision or consult others. But you simply
have to take risks."

Leadership Is ... Creativity
Born Of Adversity

—ɯ—

L et us see, first of all, what "The" Book says:

"But he knoweth the way that I take: when he hath tried me, I shall come forth as gold" (Job 23:10).

"And not only so, but we glory in tribulations also: knowing that tribulation worketh patience: And patience, experience; and experience, hope: And hope maketh not ashamed, because the love of God is shed abroad in our hearts by the Holy Ghost which is given unto us" (Romans 5:3-5).

"My brethren, count it all joy when ye fall into divers temptations, knowing this, that the trying of your faith worketh patience. But let patience have her perfect work, that ye may be perfect and entire, wanting nothing" (James 1:2-4).

Pastor Tim Cruse of Shining Light Baptist Church in Monroe, North Carolina, tells a very revealing story he heard from a tour guide while in Scotland. King George thought he would do Sir Walter Scott, the prolific but impoverished literary genius, a favor by giving him a regular support commission for the rest of his life. King George did this so Scott could concentrate on his writing without having to labor under the weight of financial pressure. The motive and intent was sincere, but the irony is that the unpressured, unstressed Scott never produced a single work of outstanding merit from that point on.

It is pressure that makes the diamond and irritation that makes the pearl.

Life handed George Washington Carver what some considered to be the skin color of disadvantage – and a handful of peanuts. Carver turned that skin color and that handful of peanuts into ingenuity that is admired the world over – and especially appreciated every time anyone has a peanut butter sandwich!

George Washington Carver (1864-1943), American botanist, the son of Negro slaves, was born near Diamond Grove, Missouri. With great tenacity he acquired a good education, receiving a B.S. in 1894 and a M.S. in 1896 from Iowa State College. From 1896 he taught and carried on research at Tuskegee Institute, especially in peanut and sweet potato culture, his discoveries bringing him international fame. From peanuts alone he derived more than 300 products, and he synthesized over 100 products from the sweet potato. His ideas helped to diversify the crops of the Southern states and to extend the use of Southern agricultural products. In 1916 he was elected a fellow of the Royal Society of Arts in London. From 1935 Carver was attached to the U.S. Department of Agriculture, and in 1940 with his life savings of $33,000 he established the Carver Foundation. Having dedicated himself wholly to his work, Carver never married. He died January 5, 1943, in Tuskegee, Alabama. On July 14th of the same year Congress authorized the creation of the George Washington Carver National Monument at his birthplace in Newton County, Missouri, and it was formally established in June, 1951.

Carver's life thoroughly exploded the idea that there is any conflict between science and religion. With him, science itself was God. He saw God in every weed he dissected in his laboratory. "Whenever I get a plant whose mysteries I want to unravel," he said, "I go into my workshop and talk to God about it, and He reveals to me the secrets."

George Washington Carver also used to say, "When I was young I said to God, 'God tell me the mystery of the universe.' But God answered, 'That knowledge is reserved for Me alone.' So I said, 'God tell me the mystery of the peanut.' Then God said, 'Well, George, that's more nearly your size.' And He told me."

In his later years Carver was invited to Washington, D.C. for a congressional hearing which attracted considerable attention. Everyone was eager to meet the modest miracle man. Influential dignitaries accompanied by reporters met the scheduled train seeking a star.

No one really noticed the gentle soul dressed in his usual ragged suit and dragging a heavy suitcase filled with dramatic experiments ready for Congress. He was lost in the crowd.

When Carver asked a redcap for assistance, the fellow looked him over quickly. "I'm sorry, Pops, but I've been sent down here to meet a very important man – a big scientist." Then before Carver could introduce himself the frantic seeker scurried away on his mission.

The modest little saint waited for the welcome committee which never found him. Finally he managed to handle his own luggage, sought his own accommodations in an African American boarding house, and later appeared on schedule before a surprised committee of Congress!

Carver's creativity was birthed out of the womb of adversity!

Adversity forces leaders to free up their minds and let their imaginations flow outside the box of conventionality.

When Douglas MacArthur's troops were battling the Chinese Communists in the Korean War, the GIs and marines seemed utterly lost, confronted by an impassable abyss; then U.S. pilots arrived overhead with a huge suspension bridge hanging from their flying boxcars and lowered it across the chasm. The soldiers crossed on the miracle span.

Wayne Gretzky, the hockey phenomenon, said, "I skate where the puck is going to be, not where it has been."

Albert Einstein said, "I think and think for months, for years. Ninety-nine times the conclusion is false. The hundredth time I am right."

In an article in *Forbes Magazine*, Frank Tyger wrote, "Discoveries are often made by not following instructions, by going off the main road, by trying the untried."

The main road is comfortable. It is also the enemy of creative leadership.

Harriet Tubman's (1820-1913) road was, perhaps, even more uncomfortable than George Washington Carver's. Her untried side road was actually under ground. It was the underground railroad! This African American hero led hundreds of slaves to freedom by ingenuity and intestinal fortitude. She never got caught and never lost a slave on any of her nineteen rescue trips. During one military campaign she helped free more than 750 slaves! At one point rewards for her capture totaled $40,000. We are told that she carried a gun and threatened to shoot any slave who tried to turn back once the journey to liberty had begun. Now that's creative leadership!

I love it. I just love it!

George Washington Carver (1864? - 1943)

Carver was born near the end of the Civil War. When he was 10, he would later recall, "God just came into my heart while I was alone in our big barn. That was my simple conversion." Carver was sent away from home at age 12 because Negroes were not allowed to attend local schools. In 1939 he was awarded the Roosevelt Medal which read, "To a scientist humbly seeking the guidance of God and a liberator to men of the white race as well as the black."

Leadership Is ... Making Your Expectations Clear To Followship

—ɷ—

Followers cannot be expected to meet expectations unless leaders make their expectations very clear. Each time the leader gives an assignment to a follower, he ought to tell the follower which of the following courses of action is expected.

a. Do it and do not report back.

b. Do it and report back immediately.

c. Do it and report regularly or routinely.

d. Investigate and make recommendations to me, and we will decide together.

e. Gather data for me, and I will decide.

Leadership Is ...
Asking The Questions
Of Wise Decision-Making

—⟋⟍—

These questions are:

Who needs to know of this decision?

Who will communicate it to those people?

Who will the decision effect?

What steps need to be taken to implement it?

Who has the responsibility for carrying out those steps?

When will the decision go into effect?

Leadership Is ...
Aware Of The Causes
Of Organizational Fragmentation

—ɯ—

These include:

1. Hard, cold, oppressive leadership – I Kings 12:13-17.

2. Unreasonable, unilateral leadership that rejects the counsel and opinions of followship without due consideration – I Kings 12:8a, 15a, 16a.

3. Selfish motives on the part of the one who is the leader – I Peter 5:3.

4. Over-lordship on the part of the one who is the leader – I Peter 5:3.

5. The rise of polarizing "personality" cults – I Corinthians 1:10-13.

6. A marked change in basic doctrine or direction – Galatians 1:6.

7.   Polarization along the lines of "gifts" or emphasis – I Corinthians 12:15-31.

8.   Carnality and the reactions of the "flesh" – I Corinthians 3:3

9.   Disrespect for the authority of the leader – Hebrews 13:7.

10.   The mistaking of egotism for leadership – III John 9.

11.   Malicious, abusive speech - III John 10a.

12.   Favoritism and factions, an "us" and "them" mentality – Acts 6:1.

13.   The preaching and legislation of preferences as convictions binding on all – Acts 15:1-2, I Timothy 1:6-10.

14.   The mishandling of the organization's monies, financial abuse – I Timothy 3:3c, 8d

15.   Disputes over affiliation – Acts 15:38.

16.   The unchecked reign of prima donna behavior – III John 10b.

Leadership Is ... Recognizing The Symptoms Of An Impending Organizational Split

—m—

These include:

1.   Internal division.

2.   Followers informally organizing cliques and factions.

3.   Increased use of voting to prove a point or make a show of "power."

4.   Long, drawn-out, personally unfulfilling meetings.

5.   Sharply increased attendance at business or policy meetings.

6.   Decreased attendance at regular meetings.

7.   Increased use of hostile language.

8.   Perceiving other followers as "enemies."

9.   Looking for conspiracies within the ranks (paranoia).

10. "We win; you lose" attitudes in decision-making.

11. Increased discussion about the goals (philosophy, direction or emphasis) of the organization indicating polarization and the breakdown of consensus.

12. Increased incongruity between what people say at public meetings and what they say privately.

13. Unfocused anxiety and anger – the "uneasy but do not know why" atmosphere.

14. An inexplicably quarrelsome climate; followers disagreeing without knowing why.

15. Physical acting out of frustrations; violent behavior behind closed doors.

16. Followers transferring to other organizations.

17. Every issue at every meeting perceived as part of the larger struggle between "us" and "them."

18. Friendship patterns change; noticeable realignment among longstanding friendships.

19. Increasing mistrust of others; increased negative labeling.

20. Evident, inexplicable pressure on the leader.

"For God hath not given us the spirit of fear; but of power and of love, and of a sound mind" (II Timothy 1:7).

-S.B. Leas, Paul Kittlaus and David M. Atkinson

Leadership Is ... Knowing How To Reduce Conflict

—m—

Genuinely spiritual leaders will never allow the Lord Jesus or the Word of God to be compromised under the guise of keeping the peace (Matthew 10:34). They will, however, endeavor to reduce conflict wherever scripturally possible (Romans 12:18).

Listed here are some methods that help to reduce conflict.

1. Learn the differences, which were previously discussed, between an authoritative leader and an authoritarian polarizer. Both types have certain characteristics in common, especially in their public, platform style. The two types will differ markedly, however, in the matter of their behind-the-scenes behavior and conduct in one-on-one relationships. The authoritative leader will wear well for years. The authoritarian type will begin to cause immediate polarization and division.

2. Reduce aggression.

3.   Refuse to entertain or be party to discussion aimed at "destroying" anyone.

4.   Emphasize room for various opinions within the framework of non-ecumenical, orthodox, Christian faith.

5.   Encourage the airing of different viewpoints; do not stifle questions or sincere inquiries about doctrine, policy, practice or finances.

6.   Do not perceive questions as threats or a challenge to your leadership.

7.   Do not be fooled into thinking that regular demands for "loyalty" will produce loyalty.

8.   Actively seek the input of any follower who seems to be withdrawing. Spend time with him.

9.   Refuse to take part in secret, manipulative planning or scheming.

10.   Deal with one issue at a time.

11.   Do not make decisions unless all involved parties are present or represented; take specific notes on all decision-making sessions; keep your notes.

12.   Do not threaten or intimidate persons or resort to the power of the "flesh" to prove your point. "Cursed be the man that trusteth in man, and maketh flesh his arm, and whose heart departeth from the Lord" (Jeremiah 17:5).

13. Deal with Bible principles rather than with personalities.

14. Know the facts; do not speak or act until you do.

15. Search for solutions that will allow the highest possible number of followers to "win" (Acts 6:2-7; Acts 15).

16. Refuse to be part of "We win; you lose" attitudes, propositions or votes.

17. Make church decisions by consensus, rather than by vote. A leader needs the good will of his followers to lead. A leader may "win" the percentage vote required by the constitution – but still lose! The percentage required by the constitution is not enough. The leader needs the consensus agreement of as many members as possible. A "forced win" is never a win – for very long!

-S.B. Leas and David M. Atkinson

Sydney Harris said, "The most important thing in an argument, next to being right, is to leave an escape hatch for your opponent, so that he can gracefully swing over to your side without too much apparent loss of face."

Leadership Is ... Susceptible To Betrayal

—m—

"And while he yet spake, behold a multitude, and he that was called Judas, one of the twelve, went before them, and drew near unto Jesus to kiss him. But Jesus said unto him, Judas, betrayest thou the Son of man with a kiss?" (Luke 22:47,48).

Not all betrayal died with Judas.

Paul wrote, "For Demas hath forsaken me, having loved this present world, and is departed unto Thessalonica" (2 Timothy 4:10).

James David Barber of Duke University wrote, "When people (followers) turn, they turn with a vengeance. The psychology of reversal can be powerful."

Sometimes followers "use" a leader much like Amnon used Tamar – for their own selfish ends. And in a strange quirk of humanity, they suddenly find that "the hatred with which they now hate the leader is greater than the love with which they loved him." See 2 Samuel 13:15.

At such times the leader and his family must find both their affirmation and comfort in the Lord Jesus Who knows the pain of betrayal and said, "I will never leave thee, nor forsake thee" (Hebrews 13:5).

Leadership Is ... Making Plans
And Provision
For Your Successor

—ɯ—

Acts 14:23 reads, "And when they had ordained them elders in every church, and had prayed with fasting, they commended them to the Lord, on whom they believed." And Paul wrote to Timothy, "Neglect not the gift that is in thee, which was given thee by prophecy, with the laying on of the hands of the presbytery" (I Timothy 4:14).

Making plans and provision for your successor is a privilege that usually falls only to a long-term leader. Short-term leaders lack the "influence" necessary to impact the selection of their successor.

It is often said that "there is no success without successors." This is a cute, little statement – and one with an element of truth. We need to also remember, however, that the Enemy of order, stability and authority also has a play book.

In Acts 20:29 and 30, the apostle Paul wrote, "For I know this, that after my departing shall grievous wolves enter in among you, not sparing the flock. Also of your own selves shall men arise, speaking perverse things, to draw away disciples after them."

Indeed, the author has observed a phenomenon over the years that seems to be a Siamese twin to the "sacrificial lamb" axiom. (The sacrificial lamb axiom says that the first new leader who comes in after a long-term, strong leader will find himself to be quite expendable after a couple of years or less.)

Eugene Kennedy, professor at Loyola University and biographer of Mayor Richard Daley of Chicago wrote:

"Great men always blur the line of succession … Anyone who claims to have a master plan after the consolidator of great power dies is a pretender … Time and chance and opportunity will have as great an effect on the choosing of his successor as anything else .. It's only afterward that people describe what happens as a plan."

In the opinion of the author, this is precisely what took place at the First Baptist Church of Dallas, Texas, when Dr. W. A. Criswell died after his fifty year ministry there. The center of momentum and power often shifts so that the one who is technically, officially and apparently the successor is not really the successor at all. The real successor, like an artesian well, springs up in another location.

It is the intent of the Enemy to thwart the "best laid plans of mice and men."

There are two equal and opposite dangers which a leader faces as he or she plans for a successor: Too little involvement in the process and too much involvement in the process. A leader should suggest and advise in the process of the selection of his successor. However, anything near a "hand-picked candidate for coronation" is liable to breed serious resentment among the followship and torpedo the candidate's prospects before he is even given a fair opportunity.

W. A. Criswell (1909 - 2002)

Wally Amos Criswell was born in Eldorado, Oklahoma. When he was 10 he trusted Christ at the close of a Wednesday morning revival service in Texline, Texas. He entered the Gospel ministry in 1928 as pastor in Marlow, Texas. In 1944 he was called to be the successor of the eminent George W. Truett at the renowned First Baptist Church of Dallas, Texas. Dr. Criswell became known as one of America's great expository preachers. He authored more than 54 books, was a leader in the rebirth of conservativism in the Southern Baptist Convention, founded two schools and pastored in Dallas for 50 years. 28,000 members were added to the church during the course of this half century of ministry. He wrote, "The big lie of our modern era is evolution … It is the cultural myth of the 20th Century."

Leadership Is ... Resisting
The Perils That Threaten

—⁂—

"... lest ... I myself should be a castaway .."
(I Corinthians 9:27)

The word "castaway" means "rejected one, one who cannot stand the test, a counterfeit, a worthless one, one who does not have the ring of truth or credibility and is therefore flung aside as irrelevant." See also Colossians 4:14, II Timothy 4:10. Spiritual leaders are threatened by perils on every side.

These "perils" have been compiled from the writings and sermons of John Henry Jowett, William A. Quayle, Charles Haddon Spurgeon, Alfred P. Gibbs and D. Martyn Lloyd-Jones. Thoughts by the author have also been interspersed.

1.   The peril of becoming personally profane (no room or enclosure for God) while engaged in and surrounded by the holy – I Samuel 2:12,16.

2.   The peril of assuming that "privilege" spells "protection."

3.   The peril of deadening familiarity with the awesome and sublime - I Samuel 2:22.

4.   The peril wherein one's "holy place" or study becomes a mechanical workshop and ceases to be an upper room.

5.   The peril of deadly familiarity with sin and its accompanying tragedies (an accustomed insensibility and callousness to the heartaches of sin and its consequences, including physical and spiritual death) - I Samuel 2:25.

6.   The peril of the possible perversion of our emotional life. The crises and stresses of service can cause the emotions to become unhealthily intense, inflammatory and neurotic. John Henry Jowett says, "A preacher's defenses are imperiled. Exaggerated emotion can be like a flood that will overwhelm and submerge his moral dykes, and plunge him into irretrievable disaster." This may have been what set the intensely emotional King David up for a fall. His fall took place when he tried to escape from the stress of battle (II Samuel 11:1). His mind and emotions were plainly seeking a diversion or release from tension and heavy, draining responsibility. Let highly emotional preachers beware. And let them deliberately plan regular times of getting away – diversion and release with their own wife and family.

7.   The peril of being inundated by emotional crises that sway the feelings and drain the soul. This leads directly to nervous impoverishment and depression which relax or lower the moral defenses and inhibitions. A preacher must insist on time "apart" which

gives space and distance from emotional crises. Some full-time counselors will take no more than four major crises situations per week! What does this say to the *pastors* who counsel plus preach plus administer?

8.   The peril of insidious, creeping love for the world which will lead to compromise and expediency under the guise of "geniality" and "sociability." This is the peril of getting absorbed into ambiguous greys under the pretext of being "all things to all men" in order to reach people. The minister of the Lord must avoid grey speech, grey humor, grey social events, grey pleasures and grey entertainment. He must realize that the gradual greying of his life and conduct will destroy his spiritual cutting edge. - Luke 6:26.

9.   The peril of losing a distinct fragrance because of spending more time with low livers than in the secret place with the Most High God. The preacher must not get so "earthy" that he no longer represents a heavenly option to people who are choking on earthiness. He must never become so much of a "jolly, good fellow" that he loses his distinctness. Leadership must offer a distinct difference or there is nothing for followers to follow.

10.   The peril of the improper stewardship of time and its resultant busyness, hurriedness, stress and bluster. John Wesley said, "I am never in a hurry, but I am always making haste." The "king's business required haste" – I Samuel 21:8.

11.   The peril of the tyranny of books - being over-awed by the "book of the hour." A stable, mature minister

will not let the new or "novel" drastically alter his direction or emphasis. Regular, pastoral visitation - either in the homes of the people or wherever most appropriate - is a good safeguard against theoretical bookishness that forgets how to relate to hurting, bleeding people.

12. The peril of fixations, obscurantism, pet peeves and hobby horses. This is the error of those who "strain at gnats and swallow camels." This is the blindness of those who cannot see the forest for the trees or, more specifically, those who cannot see the forest for the tree! (As far as they are concerned there is only <u>one</u> tree!)

13. The related peril of becoming a fanatic for the secondary and peripheral. Let us learn to be fanatics for the essentials! Let us expend our limited energies on the consequential - not the trivial or inconsequential.

14. The peril of self-deception regarding our own salvation or indispensability.

15. The peril of mistaking the seriousness of the work for the importance of our self and thus becoming our own best messiah and God's only hope in the world!

16. The peril of loving to preach but disdaining or devaluing souls.

17. The peril of inconsistent living wherein we preach one thing but do another.

18. The peril of prominence. Prominence has its perils even when it is not loved or sought. Prominence has

another set of perils when it is loved and sought (III John, verse 9).

19. The peril of unsound thinking.

20. The peril of personal financial disarray.

21. The peril of rejecting or dismissing criticism without due consideration and biblical reflection.

22. The peril of the fear of man.

23. The peril of "I owe it to myself" slothfulness and the abuse of being on "one's own honor" as to giving the work of the ministry the time it deserves.

24. The peril of selfishness.

25. The peril of the Samson complex, an "I can get away with breaking or bending the rules because God needs me" attitude - the refusal to hold self to the standards required of all believers, regardless of office or position. This occurs when power or authority inebriates the minister, and he begins to consider himself "above the law."

26. The danger of manipulating one's hearers, of continually appealing to, or, "playing to" those "hot buttons" that get a predictable response instead of getting below the plow pan of familiarity and giving people necessary (though less ear-tickling) truth.

27. The peril of perfunctory professionalism in which the externals and mechanics are fine-tuned but the heart is gone and the passion is dead.

28.   The peril of neglecting one's own, inner spiritual life – Solomon's Song 2:6c,d.

29.   The peril of an undisciplined self - an undisciplined mind or body - I Corinthians 9:27.

30.   The peril of misbehavior - I Timothy 3:15.

31.   The peril of neglecting to exercise the body (I Timothy 4:8), the conscience (Acts 24:16), the mind (Hebrews 5:14) or the spiritual life (I Timothy 4:7).

32.   The peril of the ungiven self, " ... give thyself wholly ..." - I Timothy 4:15. The work of the ministry requires self-denial, self-sacrifice and paying the price.

33.   The peril of misplaced loyalties. Our loyalty should be to Christ - not institutions, denominations, personalities or movements.

34.   The peril of the unwatched self - I Timothy 4:16.

35.   The peril of the unsaved self - I Timothy 4:16. This reference to the preacher saving himself is related not so much to the redemption of the soul as to the keeping of the soul from doctrinal and practical error.

36.   The peril of the unkept self - I Timothy 5:22c. The minister must keep himself as he would keep and tend a special garden.

37.   The peril of idols - I John 5:21.

38.   The peril of impurity - I Timothy 5:22d.

39.   The peril of getting out of the love of God - Jude 21. I do not refer, of course, to what some call "losing one's salvation." I refer to losing one's sense of God's amazing, undeserved love for sinners, the growing cold of the embers of devotion, adoration and praise.

40.   The peril of unchecked spots and blemishes in the preacher's personal character.

41.   The peril of failing to withdraw when God says, "Withdraw" - I Timothy 6:3-5.

42.   The peril of becoming overly enamored with any one leader of men or any one movement of men. Leaders are men. Men are human. Human beings are sinners. Taking in-put from several different leaders ensures opportunity for checks and balances on trends, tangents and excesses (I Corinthians 1:12-13). God seldom uses clones in an outstanding way. He usually surprises the world by using men and women who are ruggedly individualistic.

Leadership Is ... Meeting Challenges In The Power Of The Holy Spirit

—ɯ—

II Corinthians 11:23-28

Some of the challenges of ministry have faced pastors and evangelists in all ages. Others are unique to ministry in our age. I have prepared this list knowing that it is far easier to raise a problem/ issue than it is to suggest a solution. In some cases suggested solutions are found in the Scripture passages given after each point. In other cases the Scripture references are illustrations of the challenge.

1.   The challenge of resisting the pressure of "bigitis" and "the success syndrome" which stem from a lust after the praise of men – Jeremiah 5:5; I Kings 19:11-13; Zechariah 4:10.

        In a recent newsletter Dr. Ron Comfort, Evangelist and President of Ambassador Baptist College in Lattimore, North Carolina, suggested that perhaps King David's greatest sin was not the sin with Bathsheba, but rather the sin of numbering the people. Let us seek to be approved by God. Evangelist Joe B. Rice wrote the following inside the cover of his Bible, "When I speak - He shall be my theme. While I am

157

speaking - His glory shall be my goal. When I have spoken - His smile shall be my sufficient reward." The Lord "grew" Gideon's band from 22,000 to 300! – Judges 7:2.

2. The challenge to resist pragmatic thinking and planning - Romans 3:8; I Corinthians 10:31.

3. The challenge of personal purity - I Timothy 3:2; I Timothy 4:12, 16.

4. The challenge of dealing with the moral problems in the church constituency without developing a defiled mind - Galatians 6:1; Ephesians 5:11, 12.

5. The challenge of being aware of the culture without becoming "driven" by it - Acts 17:17, 18, 22, 28, 31.

6. The challenge of understanding the post-modern mind - I Corinthians 2:14-16; Colossians 2:18.

7. The challenge of the Laodicean spirit which like Korah of old resists authority in any and all forms - Revelation 3:14-17, 19; Numbers 16:1-4.

8. The challenge to resist the encroachment of secular and worldly thinking; the challenge to retain a biblical mind-set in the age of humanistic, paganistic television, videos, DVDs, internet, radio and printed matter - Romans 12:2.

9. The challenge to resist the temptation of Elijah's "I and I only am left" complex - I Kings 19:18; Romans 11:4, 5.

10.   The challenge to resist Freudian thinking and the "victim mentality" when counseling people - Genesis 3:12; Exodus 32:2, 4, 23, 24.

11.   The challenge to discern when enough counseling is enough and to know when to require how much obedience before you grant another counseling session - James 1, verses 21-24.

12.   The challenge to balance the couplets of ministry:
            a) being and doing,
            b) family and flock,
            c) private and public,
            d) discipleship and evangelism,
            e) study and administration,
            f) grace and righteousness (holiness), John 1:17; I Timothy 3:4, 5.

13.   The challenge of being personally holy without becoming an "externals only" Pharisee - Matthew 23:23-28.

14.   The challenge of pursuing excellence without imbibing the pride of perfectionism and superiority - Luke 17:10.

15.   The challenge of reaching the multi-cultural mission field at our doorstep without falling so in love with the lost that we become pluralistic and universalistic in our thinking - Acts 1:8; Ephesians 2:14; Acts 4:12.

16.   The challenge of discerning the difference between the baby and the bath water. It is often difficult to

know what to toss and what to keep - Acts 15:5, 10, 11, 19, 20.

17.   The challenge to resist being caught up in the excesses and pendulum swings of our brother preachers - II Thessalonians 2:1-3.

18.   The challenge of resisting the temptation to rely on human contacts for my security and advancement - Jeremiah 17:5; Zechariah 4:6.

        Leonard Ravenhill said, "When we wait on the Lord we renew our strength; when we wait on men we dissipate our energies."

19.   The challenge of resisting the temptation to be partisan, college-isan, camp-isan, hero-preacher-isan, or guru-isan - I Corinthians 3:3-7.

20.   The challenge of experiencing the disappointments and betrayals of the ministry without becoming a bitter cynic - Acts 20:24; II Timothy 4:10; Hebrews 12:15; Philippians 3:13, 14.

21.   The challenge of knowing when to go to "fellow-ships" and conferences and when to tend the things at home - Song of Solomon 1:6c,d; I Peter 5:2, 4.

22.   The challenge of being consistent - Galatians 2:11, 12; Luke 6:41, 42; Romans 2:1.

        This is a true story. Three equally conservative, equally ethical preachers were in a restroom during a coffee break at a "fellowship" meeting. None of them was a CCM, Christian Rock, TNIV or ecumenical crusades fellow. One preacher at a sink said to another preacher at another sink, "I am just not going to make my children memorize an archaic translation." The third preacher hidden in the stall bit his tongue to keep from responding, "But you sure don't mind using a lot of archaic music."

Consistency is probably a lot like humility. Just about the time you think you've got it, you've lost it.

23. The challenge of having a good report of those who "are without" when increasingly those without are adopting a philosophy that is opposed to everything the Bible-believer stands for - I Timothy 3:7.

24. The challenge to avoid being seduced - II Timothy 3:13; Genesis 39:7, 10.

25. The challenge of fighting a good fight without becoming a good fighter - I Timothy 6:12; II Timothy 2:24 and I Thessalonians 2:7.

It is reported that after the battle of Fredericksburg in December, 1862, Robert E. Lee remarked, "It is well that war is so terrible. We should grow too fond of it." Dwight D. Eisenhower said, "I hate war as only a soldier who has lived it can, only as one who has seen its brutality, its futility, its stupidity."

Part II

LEADERSHIP DOES NOT ...

Leadership Does Not ... Rely On Coercion

—ɯ—

"God hath made that same Jesus, whom ye have crucified, both Lord and Christ" (Acts 2:36).

Leadership has several counterfeits. There are styles of pseudo leadership that rely on brute force, domination and authoritarian control. "Leaders" who rely on these counterfeits die when their heart stops beating. Those who lead by influence live on.

Pittacus said, **"The measure of a man is what he does with power."**

Jesus is human history's greatest leader. He conquered from the vantage point of death. There will only ever be one Jesus. No one else will ever lead from the grave in the sense that He did. He arose!

However, we can safely say that all real leaders continue to lead from the grave – long after control has been surrendered. The "long shadow" of the genuine leader not only touches those who come in contact with the leader while he is alive. It also reaches beyond the grave.

Robert Murray McCheyne said, "Live so as to be missed when you are gone." As mentioned earlier, McCheyne died in his thirtieth year after only six years of ministry at St. Peter's Church in Dundee, Scotland. Yet the testimony and revival fires that his life embodied still reverberate throughout the Christian Church.

Are we so short-sighted that we are content to exercise control for the brief period we walk as a vapor on earth? Or, do we really want to lead? If we really want to lead, we will have to learn the difference between lasting leadership and temporary control.

Do you remember that General Eisenhower taught that the string can be pulled – but not pushed? Are we pulling people or are we trying to push them?

Henry Peter Brougham said, "Education makes people easy to lead, but difficult to drive."

Authoritative leadership is biblical leadership. It is based on "Thus saith the Lord." God is the ultimate authority and court of appeal.

Authoritarianism is a counterfeit.

The authoritative Christian leader says, "We need to do this in order to obey this principle which is found here in the Word of God." The authoritarian "leader" says, "Never mind, 'Why?' Don't you know who I am? Don't you know that I have connections? Do it because I say so."

The authoritative leader knows that his authority is vested in the Word of God. By contrast the authoritarian leader naively and proudly believes that his authority is vested in himself.

This kind of counterfeit leader (the authoritarian leader) brandishes and flaunts his office or position in order to force followers to comply or produce. By contrast Jesus said, "Whosoever would save his life, let him lose it" (Matthew 16:25.) And Paul wrote, "When I am weak, then am I strong" (2 Corinthians 12:10.)

In 600 B.C. Lao-tzu wrote, "Water is fluid, soft and yielding. But water will wear away rock, which is rigid and cannot yield. As a rule, whatever is fluid, soft and yielding will overcome whatever is rigid and hard. This is another paradox: what is soft is strong."

John Selden said, "They that govern the most make the least noise."

James Hudson Taylor was one of the most effective pioneer missionaries in the history of the church. Taylor wrote, "Hard missionaries are not of much use; they are not like the Master. He is never hard. It is better to be trusting and gentle and sympathetic, even if often taken in, rather than sharp and hard."

Psalm 18:35 reads, "And Thy gentleness hath made me great." In 1 Thessalonians 2:7 Paul wrote, "But we were gentle among you, even as a nurse cherisheth her children."

In his article on leadership Robert Strozier tells of self-important and newly-commissioned Major General Charles Gilbert who sternly demanded that a tired Rebel soldier salute him and succeeded only in turning the entire Rebel platoon against himself.

The "Boss" depends on his own authority. The Leader depends on maintaining good will with his followers. The "Boss" says, "Go!" The Leader says, "Let us go!"

Gerry S. Howe said, "Trust – not authority – is the pathway to results in teams."

And note well this classic quote from Pauline H. Peters. She prayed, "Lord, when I am wrong, make me willing to change; when I am right, make me easy to live with. So strengthen me that the power of my example will far exceed the authority of my rank." What a fabulous and terse expression of the difference between biblical leadership and its humanistic, carnal counterfeit!

A wise leader inspires by example. He draws like salt or a magnet. He does not fool himself into thinking that the conformity and "production" that result from heavy-handed intimidation will last when his back is turned.

John R. Mott wrote, "The strongest leaders rule by the heart. When argument and logic (and other forms of motivation) fail, they fall back on the heart."

Jesus is building His Kingdom in the *hearts* of men and women. It will be there long before it will appear in literal Jerusalem.

In 2 Thessalonians 3:7 and 9 Paul wrote, "For yourselves know how ye ought to follow us ... not because we have not power, but to make ourselves an ensample unto you to follow us."

Now what was Paul saying? He was saying that he was not going to try to get the believers at Thessalonica to follow him by coercion or "pulling rank" but rather by the salt of his influence and example. A wise leader will inspire and motivate rather than intimidate and manipulate.

Coercion is counterfeit leadership. Force and leadership are two different things. When leadership has really taken place, followers follow willingly. There is a time and a place for force, but it ought to be the exception – not the rule. We have to control children. Adults must be led.

Leadership Is Not ... The Abuse Of Power

—ᵐ—

Dr. Paul Chappell, Pastor of Lancaster Baptist Church and President of West Coast Baptist College in Lancaster, California, wrote, "I also believe there are abusive leadership styles and techniques that should be avoided if our desire is to foster an environment of servant leadership in the church. Godly leadership and authority are conferred by God and must not be grasped or seized."[15]

Leadership never exercises power for its own sake. Some imagined leaders flaunt their power because of inner insecurity and fear. Cornelius Vanderbilt boasted, "What do I care about the law? Hain't I got the power?"

Sheila Murray Bethel asks, "How do you distinguish quasi-power from real power? The characteristics are relatively easy to spot. Office holders who have only quasi-power are 'Power Pigs.' 'Power Pigs' don't admit mistakes, rarely apologize and would never ask forgiveness. They are frequently rude and discourteous. It is written: 'Rudeness is a little person's imitation of power.'"

The leader who abuses his power builds his own gallows.

Power will intoxicate the best hearts as wine the strongest heads. No man is wise enough, nor good enough, to be trusted with unlimited power.

In his article, "Litany for Dictatorships," Stephen Vincent Benét said, "We thought because we had power, we had wisdom."

Napoleon Bonaparte once said, "I ... love power. I love it as a musician loves his violin." Napoleon also believed that the first problem for a dictator is to obtain power; the second is to secure it.

However, the plain statement of Scripture in Luke 17:33 is, "Whosoever shall seek to save his life shall lose it; and whosoever shall lose his life shall preserve it."

In Shakespeare's "Julius Caesar" Brutus offers an explanation for his role in the plot against Caesar. Brutus says, "The abuse of greatness is when it disjoins remorse from power." That is power without counterbalancing humility.

In his book, *Time For Truth*, Os Guiness writes:

Traditionally, power without wisdom and virtue has been viewed as dangerous. In *The Wild Ass's Skin*, Honoré de Balzac observed that possessing power does not mean knowing how to use it. "A scepter is a toy for a child, an axe for a Richelieu, and for Napoleon a lever with which to move the earth. Power leaves our natures untouched and confers greatness only on the great."

Winston Churchill wrote similarly, reflecting on World War II, "Power, for the sake of lording it over fellow creatures or adding to personal pomp, is rightly judged base."[16]

Anne Bradstreet wrote, "Authority without wisdom is like a heavy ax without an edge: fitter to bruise than to polish."

In *The Last Days of Patton* author Ladislas Farago tells us that Hobart Richard (Hap) Gay was Patton's chief of staff. He then makes a tragic observation. General Omar Bradley thought that "Hap Gay's idol-worship of Patton ... and his uncritical acceptance of his boss actually pushed Patton even deeper into the quicksand of his bravado and the morass of his indiscretions." Many others agreed.

"Whom the gods wish to destroy they first make mad." Mad with power.

Peter Green writes,

"Alexander the Great had his special envoy Nicanor – Aristotle's adopted son – take a second decree with him for announcement at the Olympic Games. It required that the cities of the League would publicly acknowledge him as a god.

"Whatever his divination meant to anyone else, Alexander himself took it very seriously indeed. Year by year, with growing isolation that is the penalty of an unbroken ascent to absolute power, Alexander's control over his own latent megalomania had grown progressively weaker. He took refuge from the insecurity of power in the greater exercise of power: like a god intervening in the affairs of mortals, he would order the fate of princes and nations.

"He became a god when he ceased wholly to trust his powers as a man, taking the divine shield of invincibility to combat his inner fear of failure. He was formidable still: but he had come very near the end of the road."

The man who adopts the guise of godhood through the abuse of power is revealing his own desperate insecurity! Abusive power fails to advocate both the *glory of God* and the *good of followers* and makes decision solely for reasons of self-preservation and self-perpetuation.

Back in the mid 1970's when his monthly publication was printed only in black ink on pastel paper, I read something from the pen of Charles R. Swindoll that kept me out of a lot of hot water. I here quote the piece verbatim:

"Some seek church leadership for the wrong reason. They want to take charge so that they can get their own way. They want to be in a position of authority so they can hold others in check or force them to get in line. Though some accomplish this as masters of deceit, hiding the real truth behind smiling masks and pious words, their domineering style becomes evident when those who are supposed to follow don't … when they exert some healthy and creative independence. "Anathema!" cries the ruler. "Zap!" **Power people have little tolerance for folks who think on their own and speak their mind.**

"For some strange reason the religious ranks are swollen with those who have yielded to this particular temptation. Give certain people enough authority to lead, a Bible to quote, and *a need to succeed* … and before long you'd think Caesar had been reincarnated. It is no surprise that Peter, when addressing those who shepherd the flock of God, warned against lording it over those allotted to your charge (I Peter 5:3). Power-mad leaders leave more battered sheep than we would ever believe. And the special tragedy of that is that battered sheep seldom fully recover."

There are leaders who gorge themselves on power because they are addicted to it. It is their adrenalin rush.

Os Guinness writes that Picasso was often a monster in his relationships – especially with women – because of his controlling, devouring personality. He once declared, "When I die it will be a shipwreck, and as when a big ship sinks, many people all around will be sucked down with it."[16]

General Patton was convinced that he surpassed Napoleon, the Little Corporal, in brilliance. He told his son, "(Napoleon) and I fought the same battle, but my means of progress were better than his." To a friend in Boston he wrote, "My private opinion is that practically everybody but myself is a pusillanimous (expletive deleted)."

When Patton did not get the transfer he wanted from the European theater to the Japanese theater he blamed the disappointment on the fact that his style was too fast for the Japanese theater! In actuality any discussion about his style had simply been a smoke-screen to camouflage the fact that Douglas MacArthur had categorically rejected both him and his services. A power-hungry ego just never quite gets it.

Oswald Chambers said, "Unguarded strength is double weakness."

An unknown writer said, "He sits not sure that sits too high."

Mark Antony said, "Only Antony can conquer Antony." And he did.

Hubris is a nemesis that has brought down the strongest of leaders. Dryden said, "Even victors are by victory undone."

In the book of Esther, the Bible tells of Haman who became very powerful. In chapter 3, verses 1 and 2 we read, "After these things did king Ahasuerus promote Haman ... and advanced him, and set his seat above the princes that were with him. And all the king's servants, that were in the king's gate, bowed, and reverenced Haman: for the king had so commanded concerning him." But Haman was not content with that. He was displeased with one person, Mordecai, and built gallows planning to hang Mordecai with the king's permission. In the end, however, Haman overstepped his power. We learn the result in Esther 7:10, "So they hanged Haman on the gallows that he had prepared for Mordecai. Then was the king's wrath pacified."

I repeat, the leader who abuses his power builds his own gallows.

Leadership Does Not ... Fail To Identify With Followers

—⟋⟍⟍—

We read in I John 1:1-3, "That which was from the beginning, which we have heard, which we have seen with our eyes, which we have looked upon, and our hands have handled, of the Word of life; (For the life was manifested, and we have seen it, and bear witness, and shew unto you that eternal life, which was with the Father, and was manifested unto us;) That which we have seen and heard declare we unto you, that ye also may have fellowship with us and truly our fellowship is with the Father, and with his Son Jesus Christ."

Leadership must spend time with followship.

In Ezekiel 3:15 the prophet tells us that he "came to them of the captivity at Tel-abib ... and I sat where they sat, and remained there astonished among them seven days." Ezekiel got out among the captives and entered into their situation.

Hebrews 4:15 reminds us that we "have not an high priest which cannot be touched with the feeling of our infirmities; but was in all points tempted like as we are ..."

Leaders who have identified with their followers have earned the right to lead. The ivory tower commanders create their own resentment and opposition.

On September 13, 1940, Queen Elizabeth, the Queen Mother, told a London policeman, "I'm glad we've been bombed. It makes me feel I can look the East End in the face."

When it was suggested that the royal family be evacuated during the Nazi Blitz, the Queen Mother replied, "The Princesses would never leave without me, and I couldn't leave without the King, and the King will *never* leave."

Identification with the milieu and circumstance of followship's reality endears leadership to followship. The incarnation of the Lord Jesus is the most obvious, profound and powerful illustration of this principle.

King David's failure to be out in the field of combat where his soldiers were is forever associated with the nadir of his nobility, respectability and effectiveness. The comforts and securities of home beckoned him but the battlefield was the critical point at that moment. (2 Samuel 11:1) How different from David was Uriah who refused the opportunity to go home and insisted on remaining with his men!

On one occasion Stonewall Jackson also refused to take leave to see his wife and daughter because his men could not do the same.

General Willard W. Scott, Jr., Superintendent of the United States Military Academy expressed this principle as an absolute. He said, "You've got to find the critical point. And be there."

The Bible says of Jesus Christ in John 1:14, **"The Word was made flesh and dwelt among us."**

There are many times when the leader's "just showing up" earns a lifetime of loyal affection from his followers. Pastors must learn that faithful hospital visitation and in-person-ministry in the time of crisis are essential. Leaders must be sensitive to the "tender points" of followship and ... be there.

Many years ago my Work of the Ministry professor who was also a pastor told our class how he had lovingly rebuked his Assistant because the Assistant had insisted on keeping his pre-arranged plan to go out of town and buy peaches when a church member was taken to the hospital critically ill. Our professor declared, "The peaches have to wait. The point of need must come first."

Plutarch records that "Caesar implanted and nurtured high spirits and ambition in his men by willingly exposing himself to every danger and shrinking from no hardship."

General Ernest D. Peixotto wisely observed, "You can't let yourself be captured by the in-box ... You've got to go out in the trenches. In combat, it means going to the guy who's actually out there in the foxhole and finding out what's going on ... You (must) get a feel for how the organization operates."

This feel only comes from enfleshment, sitting where they sit.

Robert Murray M'Cheyne insisted on visiting his parishioners during the typhus fever plague in Dundee, Scotland, in 1843 despite the fact that his own body was in a weakened state. He contracted the plague and died before his thirtieth birthday after only six years as St. Peter's pastor. Myopic vision says, "What a waste!" but R.M. M'Cheyne's example of incarnational ministry continues to transform "followers" to this day.

P.T. Forsyth said, "You must live with people to know their problems, and live with God in order to solve them."

In his masterpiece entitled *If* Rudyard Kipling wrote:

If you can talk with crowds and keep your virtue,
Or walk with kings – nor lose the common touch,
If neither foes nor loving friends can hurt you,
If all men count with you, but none too much;
If you can fill the unforgiving minute
With sixty seconds' worth of distance run,
Yours is the Earth and everything that's in it,
And – which is more – you'll be a Man, my son!

Kipling understood that the earth belongs to those who can <u>both</u> "talk with crowds" <u>and</u> "walk with kings."

In *Stonewall Jackson*, author Allen Tate tells us that on January 5, 1862, General Loring's division was at the point of mutiny because they had marched over ice-covered roads, had no tents and no close access to their supply wagons, "Jackson was not sympathetic with their complaints. He had one fixed idea: The success of the Southern cause. Hunger and cold were nothing.

"One morning some members of the Stonewall Brigade, rising, shook off the blanket of snow that had thoughtfully come down upon them while they slept. They cursed the leader that had let them suffer. They said he was mad. The whole expedition was insane. Then they saw a not unfamiliar figure get up and shake off his snow-blanket; the figure approached them. He called out a pleasant "Good morning!" He had been lying only a few feet away and he had heard them.

"What kind of man was General Jackson? He had not uttered a word of sympathy for their suffering. He had issued harsh and peremptory orders. But he suffered exactly as they did."

The Preacher's Mistake

The parish priest
Of austerity,
Climbed up a high church steeple
To be nearer to God,
So that he might hand
His word down to his people.

When the sun was high,
When the sun was low,
The good man sat unheeding
Sublunary things.
From transcendence
Was he forever reading.

And now and again
When he heard the creak
Of the weather vane a-turning,
He closed his eyes
And said, "Of a truth
From God I am now learning."

And in sermon script
He daily wrote
What he thought was sent from heaven,
And he dropped this down
On his people's heads
Two times one day in seven.

In his age God said,
"Come down and die!"
And he cried out from the steeple,
"Where art thou, Lord?"
And the Lord replied,
"Down here among my people."

-William Croswell Doane

Michael Reagan, the conservative commentator and adopted son of President Ronald Reagan, tells a very moving story that illustrates how a genuine leader identifies with followship.

In the 1976 U.S. presidential primary race Ronald Reagan was campaigning in North Carolina. Someone came up to one of his staff members and said, "I have some blind children here who would like to meet Governor Reagan. They were about 9 or 10 years old. There were about ten kids. My father overheard that and said that instead of bringing these children up in the lights of the camera and using them, "Just take them back to my trailer and I will talk to them in the privacy of my trailer." My dad went to the trailer to meet with these kids. (Dana Rohrbacher tells this story because he was there. He was a speechwriter for my dad at the time.) And Dana says that my dad was there talking to these kids and, all of a sudden, the light goes on in my father's mind that these kids can't see him. So, my dad says to these kids, "Would you like to touch my face?" And Dana says that all these kids came over, and dad got down on his knees, and these children just touched his face. And I think that really tells the story.[17]

Ronald Reagan (1911 - 2004)

Ronald Wilson Reagan was born in Tampico, Illinois, population 820. His mother excelled at "readings," dramatic or humorous passages from poems, plays or speeches and introduced him to the exhilaration of public speaking. By his senior year his secret dream to be an actor was firmly established. The door to the fulfillment of this dream opened when he was hired to be a sportscaster at Radio WOC, Davenport, Iowa. Mr. Reagan went on to have leading roles in more than 50 films over a span of 30 years. Following an 8 year stint as host of the General Electric Theater Hour he was elected governor of California. He became the 40th President of the U.S. when he defeated Jimmy Carter in 1980. He was reelected in 1984, winning 525 electoral votes – more than any other presidential candidate in U.S. history.

Leadership Does Not ...
Try To Operate
In An Information Vacuum Or
A Milieu Which Ignores Experience

—⟋⟍—

 uch folly is a sin of pride.

Solomon's son, Rehoboam, split the once glorious kingdom of Israel because "he forsook the counsel of the old men" who had told him to approach leadership with a "be a servant to be served" spirit (I Kings 12:6, 7). Rehoboam relegated both the information and the discretion of experience to the museum of irrelevancy. And followship suffered immensely.

When Stephen Harper was elected as one of the youngest prime ministers in the history of Canada in January, 2006, he faced the daunting task of drawing both his own political party and his nation back toward the center. The country – and all the political parties in the country – had been wallowing in the mire of self-indulgent liberalism and socialism since Prime Minister John Diefenbaker had been forced from office in 1963.

Most pundits said Harper's government would self-destruct within a year. He had come to power as an outsider with widely publicized Christian roots in a nation that had demonstrated tolerance for every group but Christians for twenty years.

I saw hope for Mr. Harper and his government when he reached way back to the 1980's government of Prime Minister Mulroney and tapped key personnel from that era for both his transition team and his cabinet. He had won the election with little assistance (and some criticism) from them, but he was wise enough and humble enough to know that even though he differed with the philosophy of the so-called "pink Tories," he could learn the ropes of governing from them. Harper's critics expected hard-line, youthful arrogance, independence and self-sufficiency from the "outsider" from renegade Western Canada. But Harper confounded the prophets and, to quote the poet, Edwin Markham, he "drew a circle that drew them in." He surprised the experts of all parties who predicted that Harper would be so unteachable that he would destroy himself within months.

It is mature, secure leadership that is not threatened by either information or seasoned experience. He who will not learn from the hoary head will soon lose his own head.

Leadership Does Not ... Allow Itself To Be Pressured Or Panicked Into Unilateral And Possibly Ill-Informed Decision-Making

—ↄ—

In Acts 15 we read of a situation in the early church where a question of policy came up between believing Jews and believing Gentiles. Representatives came before the leaders of the church in Jerusalem, and verse 6 tell us, "And the apostles and elders came together for to consider of this matter."

It is acceptable to announce a decision or policy that is unpopular. Abraham Lincoln had to do this on several occasions. Leadership involves making tough calls. However, it is not wise to reach the decision unilaterally or in ignorance, that is, without asking for any input from followers. If you are going to have opposition, you would be wise to know from which flank it will come.

Input may add only a slight modification to your decision, but it just might be that slight modification or "tweak" that saves the day.

"For by wise counsel thou shalt make thy war: and in multitude of counselors there is safety" (Proverbs 24:6).

Leadership Does Not ...
Remain Blind
To Its Own Strengths And
Weaknesses

—ᘺ—

Peter Drucker said, "Strong people always have strong weaknesses." Drucker's statement immediately brings Paul's declaration in II Corinthians 12:9-10 to mind. The similarity between these two statements is uncanny. Paul said, "For when I am weak, then am I strong."

Oswald Chambers wrote, "An unguarded strength is a double weakness."

Philip M. McDonald speaks of "the peril of self-deception." Romans 12:3 reads, "For I say, through the grace given unto me, to every man that is among you, not to think of himself more highly than he ought to think, but to think soberly, according as God hath dealt to every man the measure of faith."

What is humility? It is certainly not gainsaying or demeaning the abilities, talents and blessings God has given us. Humility is stepping back for an objective, realistic view of ourselves and giving God all the glory for anything positive we see. I Corinthians 4:7 says, "For who maketh thee to differ from another? and what hast thou that thou didst not receive? Now if thou didst receive it, why dost thou glory, as if thou hadst not received it?" We can never be totally objective about ourselves for "the heart is deceitful above all things, and desperately wicked" (Jeremiah 17:9).

Dwight D. Eisenhower wrote, "Humility must always be the portion of any man who receives acclaim earned in the blood of his followers and the sacrifices of his friends."

With the help of trusted family members, friends and coworkers we can analyze our God-given equipment and develop it as good stewards of "the manifold [multi-faceted] grace of God." As we gain insight into our strengths and weaknesses, we must remember: A strength abused can quickly become a fatal weakness, and a weakness resented can quickly paralyze with bitterness; a weakness accepted can be turned into a powerful life mission.

Strengths and weaknesses are a lot like victories and defeats. None of them are necessarily final. The seeds of weakness grow in our strengths, and the seeds of strength grow in our weaknesses.

God does not give us strengths so that we can become stuck on ourselves. He gives us strengths so that we can enrich the lives of people around us. The leader who becomes "stuck on" or "turned in upon" himself will eat himself up. The leader whose cause degenerates into perpetuating a cult of self will destroy everything he worked for in earlier, more self-less days. Proverbs 16:18 reads, "Pride goeth before destruction, and an haughty spirit before a fall."

The Greville Diary of 1927 declares that the "(Duke of) Wellington was without a particle of vanity or conceit ... He never seemed aware of universal adulation."

G.K. Chesterton said, "There is the (so-called) 'great' man who makes every man feel small. But the real great man is the man who makes every man feel great."

In his book *American Caesar* William Manchester made the following observations about General Douglas MacArthur, "If MacArthur is to be seen in the round, the magnitude of this viceregal triumph (as the representative of Allied powers in post-World War II Japan) ... must be grasped and understood as an expression of the very hub of his character. During his lifetime, his admirers saw only his victories; his critics saw only his defeats. What neither appreciated was that identical traits led to his winnings and his losses. His hauteur, his willingness to defy superiors, his fascination with the political process, his contempt for vacillation – these would be his undoing in the end. But along the way they reaped historic fruit. There can be no doubt that they made a great democracy of Japan."

The May 13, 1962, issue of *The New York Times* quoted Dwight D. Eisenhower as saying, "Each of us has his portion of ego. At least one night I dreamed that the 22nd amendment (limiting a president to two terms) had been repealed – and it wasn't wholly a nightmare."

Leaders do not let a promotion go to their head. Upon being congratulated by the press on being promoted to Brigadier-General, Ike said, "When they get clear down to my place on the list, they are passing out stars with considerable abandon."

J. Oswald Sanders wrote, "Leaders who stay the course are kept from over-reaching or self-destruction by living in the humility of a great repentance regarding self. They have a realistic remorse over their own weaknesses and sins."

John R. Rice (1895 - 1980)

He was dedicated to the Lord before his birth, and his mother referred to him as "my preacher boy." Though she died before he was 6, her son certainly fulfilled her desire. A successful evangelistic campaign in Oak Cliff, Texas, in 1932 led to the establishment of a Baptist church. Here America's foremost conservative newspaper, *The Sword of the Lord*, was born. With spiritual revival as its theme, the publication has reached a circulation of millions.

Leadership Does Not ...
Get So Involved
With The Mechanics Of
Administration That It Neglects The
Essentials Of Its Own Personal Walk
With God:
Prayer, Bible Reading, Holiness And
Soulwinning

—⁄⁄⁄—

We can see this in the following verses from Scripture. I Thessalonians 5:17, "Pray without ceasing." Psalm 119:11, "Thy word have I hid in mine heart, that I might not sin against thee." And Proverbs 11:30, "The fruit of the righteous is a tree of life, and he that winneth souls is wise."

General Robert E. Lee wrote:

"Knowing that intercessory prayer is our mightiest weapon and the supreme call for all Christians today, I pleadingly urge our people everywhere to pray. Believing that prayer is the greatest contribution that our people can make in this critical hour, I humbly urge that we take time to pray – to really pray.

"Let there be prayer at sunup, at noonday, at sundown, at midnight – all through the day. Let us pray for our children, our youth, our aged, our pastors, our homes. Let us pray for our churches.

"Let us pray for ourselves, that we may not lose the word 'concern' out of our Christian vocabulary. Let us pray for our nation. Let us pray for those who have never known Jesus Christ and redeeming love, for moral forces everywhere, for our national leaders. Let prayer be our passion. Let prayer be our practice."

Stonewall Jackson loved to walk and pray at the same time. He found that advantageous to both body and soul.

Jackson told his pastor, Dr. White, that he had found nothing in the Scriptures prohibiting prayer with open eyes. He said, "Every thought should be a prayer. The attitude of prayer should become a habit."

Dr. Oswald J. Smith of The People's Church in Toronto, Canada, often paced back and forth as he prayed.

The leader who never prays is either a supreme egotist, a humanist or a practical atheist – or all three.

How sad that a leader would be so small.

In spite of what is widely known regarding General Patton's unbecoming profanity, H. Essame says that "both Patton and Montgomery believed profoundly in the efficacy of prayer as an aid to victory."

When Stonewall Jackson took gravely ill after the loss of his left arm, Robert E. Lee sent the following message, "When a suitable occasion offers, give him my love, and tell him that I wrestled in prayer for him last night, as I have never prayed, I believe for myself."

General Eisenhower, surrounded by his staff officers, stood on a high hill overlooking Malta harbor. In the light of a full moon shining down on the sea he watched the troop laden ships weigh anchor and sail out into the mists while squadrons of planes roared into the sky. Deeply moved, Eisenhower sprang to attention and saluted his heroic men. Then he bowed his head in silent prayer, his staff joining him in this brief act of devotion. Turning to an officer beside him, Eisenhower said, "There comes a time when you've used your brains, your training, your technical skill, and the die is cast. The events are in the hands of God, and there you have to leave them."

In a letter to his son, George Washington said, "Remember that God is our only sure trust. To Him, I commend you ... My son, neglect not the duty of secret prayer."

In his Inaugural Address, January 21, 1957, President Dwight D. Eisenhower exclaimed, "Before all else, we seek upon our common labor as a nation, the blessings of Almighty God. And the hopes in our hearts fashion the deepest prayers of our whole people."

John R. Rice wrote, "Many of us cannot get our prayers heard because the cry of another whom we have wronged has already been heard by God. Cain tried to talk to God, but the blood of his brother Abel had already cried out of the ground to God."

Leadership Does Not ... Try To Do The Work Of The Spirit In The Strength Of The Flesh

—ɯ—

We find written in Galatians 3:3, "Are ye so foolish? having begun in the Spirit, are ye now made perfect by the flesh?" and in I Corinthians 3:3, "For ye are yet carnal: for whereas there is among you envying, and strife, and divisions, are ye not carnal, and walk as men?"

Dr. Clarence Sexton wrote, "Not long before he died, Dr. Curtis Hutson preached one of his greatest sermons. He preached on the difference between sailing and rowing. He used the analogy of allowing the Spirit of God to get in our sail, taking us where He leads, or rowing and rowing in our own strength. Dr. Hutson said, 'I have rowed nearly all of my life. Nearly all of my life I have tried to make it happen.' He said, 'I want to spend the rest of it sailing.'" Are you rowing or sailing?

Toshikazu Kaze, the diminutive Japanese diplomat, was a graduate of Amherst and Harvard and secretary to the Foreign Minister. He was present and prepared the official report on the ceremony in which the Japanese surrendered to General MacArthur on the ship, Missouri, September 2,

1945, for his emperor Hirohito. He wrote as follows, "We were not beaten on the battlefield by dint of superior arms. We were defeated in the spiritual contest by virtue of a nobler idea. The real issue was moral – beyond all the power of algebra to compute."

Dr. Greg Baker, Pastor of FaithWay Baptist Church and President of FaithWay Baptist College in Ajax, Ontario, said, "We were traveling along the California coast and watched some men preparing to go surfing. I thought about these facts: You can buy the most expensive surfboard; you can wax that board with the most expensive wax; you can be trained by the best surfing instructor in all the world; you can be in the best physical condition to be able to withstand the physical strain of having those waves beat upon you … but what you really need if you are going to be an effective surfer … is a wave! Now I want to ask you, aren't you tired of trying to manufacture a wave in your church? Listen, only God can create a wave. It's not by might. It's not by power, but it's by My Spirit, saith the Lord (Zechariah 4:6)."

Dwight D. Eisenhower stated, "The spirit of man is more important than mere physical strength, and the spiritual fiber of a nation than its wealth."

In his broadcast to the American people immediately following the signing of the instrument of surrender by the Japanese in Tokyo Bay on September 2, 1945, General Douglas MacArthur said, "Men since the beginning of time have sought peace, but military alliances, balances of power, leagues of nations, all in turn failed, leaving the only path to be by way of the crucible of war … Now we have had our last chance. If we do not now devise some greater and more equitable system, Armageddon will be at our door. The problem basically is theological and requires a spiritual recrudescence [renewal, reawakening] and improvement of human character that will synchronize with our almost matchless advances in science, art, literature and all material and cultural developments of the past 2000 years. **It must be of the spirit if we are to save the flesh.**"

Leadership Does Not ... Assume That Followship Silence Necessarily Means Followship Approval

—ɷ—

Wise followers know that there is " ... a time to keep silence, and a time to speak" (Ecclesiastes 3:7b).

Wise leaders must learn to interpret both.

Leadership Does Not ... Commit The 8 Deadly Sins Which Destroy A Leader's Credibility

—⟋⟋⟍—

What are the eight deadly sins?

a. Over explanation, giving information that raises unnecessary issues.

b. Breach of confidentiality.

c. Lack of communication.

d. Harsh response.

e. Inaccessibility. Telephone answering machines and voice mail are often offensive to followship who begin to think that leaders use these items of technology to avoid direct contact with them.

f. Passivity or timidity.

g. The fear of man or conflict with man.

h. The inordinate desire to please man.

Leadership Does Not ... Believe That "Failure" Is Final

—ɯ—

William Arthur Ward said, "Failure is not fatal. Failure should be our teacher, not our undertaker ... From honest failure can come valuable experience."

Thomas Edison said, "A failure teaches you that something can't be done – that way."

"It took me fifteen years to discover I had no talent for writing, but I couldn't give it up because by that time I was too famous," said Robert Benchley.

George Bernard Shaw commented, "When I was a young man I observed that nine out of ten things I did were failures. I didn't want to be a failure, so I did ten times more work."

Edison did not give up when his first efforts to find an effective filament for the carbon incandescent lamp failed. He did countless experiments with countless kinds of materials. As each failed, he would toss it out the window. The pile reached to the second story of his house. Then he sent men to China, Japan, South America, Asia, Jamaica, Ceylon and Burma in search of fibers and grasses to be tested in his laboratory.

One weary day on October 21, 1879 – after thirteen months of repeated failures – he succeeded in his search for a filament that would stand the stress of electric current. This was how it happened:

Casually picking up a bit of lampblack, he mixed it with tar and rolled it into a thin thread. Then the thought occurred: Why not try a carbonized cotton fiber? For five hours he worked, but it broke before he could remove the mold. Two spools of thread were used up. At last a perfect strand emerged – only to be ruined when trying to place it in a glass tube. Edison refused to admit defeat. He continued without sleep for two days and nights. Finally he managed to slip one of the carbonized threads into a vacuum-sealed bulb. And he turned on the current. "The sight we had so long desired to see finally met our eyes."

His persistence amidst such discouraging odds has given the world the amazing electric light!

One of Edison's light bulbs – the one hung in the Livermore, California Fire Department, was turned on in 1901 and burned almost constantly for 71 years. By our standards, it should have burned out 852 times.

Plato wrote the first sentence of his famous *Republic* nine different ways before he was satisfied.

Bryant rewrote one of his poetic masterpieces 99 times before publication, and it became a classic.

Burke wrote the conclusion of his speech at the trial of Hastings sixteen times.

Butler rewrote his famous *Analogy* twenty times.

Virgil spent seven years on his *Georgica* and twelve on the *Aeneid*. Nevertheless, he was so displeased with the latter that he tried to rise from his deathbed to throw the manuscripts into the flames.

In the British Museum one can see 75 drafts of Thomas Gray's, *Elegy Written in a Country Churchyard.*

Beethoven is unsurpassed in his painstaking fidelity to his music. Hardly a bar of his was not written and rewritten at least a dozen times.

Michelangelo's *Last Judgment*, one of the twelve master paintings of the ages, was the product of eight years of unremitting toil. Over 2,000 studies of it were found among his papers.

Burbank, the plant wizard, personally conducted over 6,000 experiments before finding the solution he sought. And Westinghouse was treated as a mild lunatic by most railroad executives. "Stopping a train by wind! The man's crazy!" Yet he persevered and finally sold the air-brake idea.

Bernard Montgomery, the British general said, "No man ever made war so horribly as Caesar did in Gaul."

Stonewall Jackson failed to promptly attack at Mechanicsville and Gaines' Mill and delayed inexplicably in crossing White Oak Swamp.

Wendell Phillips said, "Defeat is nothing but the first step toward something higher."

"Our greatest glory is not in never falling but in rising every time we fall," said Oliver Goldsmith.

Goethe wrote, "Daring ideas are like chessman moved forward; they may be beaten, but they may start a winning game."

When Ronald Reagan lost the nomination for President to Gerald Ford in 1976 he quoted an old Scottish poem:

> I am wounded – but not slain
> I will lay me down and rest awhile
> And rise to fight another day.

Leadership Does Not ... Assume That Criticism Is A Threat

—ɯɯ—

Leadership does not assume that person-to-person, face-to-face criticism is intended as a threat to one's leadership. "A reproof entereth more into a wise man than an hundred stripes into a fool ... Faithful are the wounds of a friend; but the kisses of an enemy are deceitful" (Proverbs 17:10 and 27:6).

It was a very secure General Eisenhower who said, "If we allow ourselves to be persuaded that every individual or party that takes issue with our own convictions is necessarily wicked or treasonous, then, indeed, we are approaching the end of freedom's road."

The "Book" has something to say regarding the fear of critics. "The fear of man bringeth a snare: but whoso putteth his trust in the Lord shall be safe" (Proverbs 29:25). "The Lord is my light and my salvation; whom shall I fear? The Lord is the strength of my life; of whom shall I be afraid? When the wicked, even mine enemies and my foes, came upon me to eat up my flesh, they stumbled and fell. Though an host should encamp against me, my heart shall not fear: though war should rise against me, in this will I be confident ... In God I will praise his word, in God I have put my trust;

I will not fear what flesh can do unto me" (Psalm 27:1-3 and 56:4).

General Omar N. Bradley declared, "If a soldier would command an army he must be prepared to withstand those who would criticize the manner in which he leads that army."

Leadership assumes criticism; the leader must be mature enough and wise enough to winnow criticism, keeping the wheat and blowing the chaff away.

A man who wants to lead the orchestra must turn his back on the crowd.

Abraham Lincoln said, "If I were to read, much less answer, all the attacks made on me, this shop might as well be closed for any other business. I do the very best I know – the very best I can; and I mean to keep doing so until the end. If the end brings me out all right, what is said against me won't amount to anything. If the end brings me out wrong, the angels swearing I was right would make no difference."

General Eisenhower wrote to Omar Bradley and said, "Dear Brad ... If you are going to do anything constructive someone is going to attack you; I do hope you will never let such inconsequential things worry you ... Don't defend yourself – Don't explain – Don't worry!!"

There are two quick ways to disaster: Taking nobody's advice and taking everybody's advice. A leader must be willing to be unpopular when necessary. Winston Churchill said, "Leadership means not having to be completely in harmony with everyone else."

Churchill and Teddy Roosevelt certainly shared that indomitable spirit that made them two of the most refreshing figures to walk across the stage of modern history. When he was at The Sorbonne on April 23, 1910, Roosevelt said, "It is not the critic who counts. The credit belongs to the man who is actually in the arena; whose face is marred by the sweat and blood; who strives valiantly; who errs and comes short again and again; because there is no effort without error and shortcoming. But he who actually does strive to do the deeds, who knows the great enthusiasms, the great devotions, who spends himself in a worthy cause, who at the best knows in the end the triumphs of high achievement and who, at the worst, if he fails, at least fails while daring greatly, so that his place shall never be with those cold and timid souls who know neither victory nor defeat."

One leader who must have felt rather "pounced upon" left us a very apt metaphor for the criticism which automatically comes to leaders. He wrote, "This is what it is like for a man to be in authority: Children at play don't even bother to look for a ball that is punctured. It can stay with tranquility in a corner. But when it is pumped up the children jump out from all sides and everyone believes that he has the right to kick it. This is what happens to men when they move up. Do not, therefore, be envious of a place of leadership."

When someone questioned his conversion because he did not quite fit into either of the two major "camps" of Baptists, Charles H. Spurgeon wrote to a friend, "I am not very easily put down. I go right on and care for no man on God's earth."

Leaders should expect to be criticized and not fear the criticism when it comes.

George Whitefield (1714 - 1770)

As a boy he lived above the Bell's Inn at Gloucester, England, and helped his mother serve the guests their "refreshment" down below. He soon became attached to the art of acting and the stage. However, by the time he entered Oxford University in 1732 he began to have "scruples" about theater life. Soon he began to meet with John and Charles Wesley in what was dubbed as the "Holy Club." After a month of fasting, self-denial and exhaustion, Whitefield cast himself on the mercy of God and "a full assurance of faith broke upon his soul." Between 1736 and 1770 he preached more than 18,000 sermons to crowds in Britain and the American colonies.

Leadership Does Not ...Forget That It Must Be A Mastermind

—〰〰—

We read in Song of Solomon 2:15, "Take us the foxes, the little foxes, that spoil the vines: for our vines have tender grapes." And then we read what Paul wrote to Titus, "For this cause left I thee in Crete, that thou shouldest set in order the things that are wanting, and ordain elders in every city, as I had appointed thee" (Titus 1:5).

A mastermind is a mind that accesses details and information from every pertinent and available source. Henry Ford built the Ford Motor Company on the principle of the mastermind. He knew he was not knowledgable in many areas of expertise required to build an automobile, but he assembled a team of experts in these fields and moved them to Detroit. They were as close to him as the intercom on his desk. Ford knew which button to push for the question at hand. The "details" expert was there in a flash and Ford had his answer.

The National Aeronautics and Space Administration warns that "the smallest speck of dust in the controls may cause a major deviation of thousands of miles of the space shuttle."

The wise leader knows that the "catch" or "rub" is in the details. Or, is it the Devil? He also realizes that he cannot possibly master all the details of every facet of his work, so he learns whose knowledge or wisdom to tap in a given situation or problem. And he does not hesitate to do so!

Leaders do not obsess over details. (They ask others to do that and hold them accountable.) Leaders keep their eyes on the big picture – and save their energies for the big picture. They concern themselves more with how the smaller parts relate to the larger whole.

General Eisenhower paid General Omar N. Bradley a great compliment. He said, "Everything (Bradley) does is accomplished in such a manner as to fit in well with all the other operations."

Troy Middleton said, "Bradley considered all the angles."

Leadership Does Not ... Make Too Many Changes Before Winning The Respect Of Followers

—ɯ—

Making too many changes before winning the respect of followers, making changes without thinking through and preparing for the implications of the changes is not wise. Proverbs 24:21 tells us, "My son, fear thou the Lord and the king: and meddle not with them that are given to change."

Conservatives, by nature, resist change. Changes that are unscriptural are bad – morally bad. There are other kinds of changes that are good.

If the leader communicates information and sound reasoning to his followers he can gradually prepare them *in advance* for change and thereby avoid what Millard Macadam calls "toxic" reactions "that kill productivity."

Leadership Does Not ... Retaliate Against Those Who Are Perceived To Be A Threat

—m—

Leaders should not retaliate against those who are perceived to be a threat to their position. "Dearly beloved, avenge not yourselves, but rather give place unto wrath: for it is written, Vengeance is mine; I will repay, saith the Lord" (Romans 12:19).

Pastor Ervin McNeill, the Chaplain of Pacific Garden Mission in Chicago, speaks of a truth he was taught many years ago. It goes like this: Nothing promises so much and delivers so little as revenge.

The late Dr. A.T. Pierson told the following story of General Robert E. Lee. Hearing General Lee speak in the highest terms to President Jefferson Davis about a certain Confederate officer, another officer, greatly astonished, said to him, "General, do you not know that the man of whom you spoke so highly to the President is one of your bitterest enemies, and misses no opportunity to malign you?" "Yes," replied General Lee, "but the President asked my opinion of him, and I gave him a true answer. He did not ask his opinion of me."

Leadership Does Not ... Fail To Delegate Responsibility

—w—

A good example of delegating responsibility is found in Ephesians 4:11-13, "And he gave some, apostles; and some, prophets; and some, evangelists, and some, pastors and teachers; For the perfecting of the saints, for the work of the ministry, for the edifying of the body of Christ: Till we all come in the unity of the faith, and of the knowledge of the Son of God, unto a perfect man, unto the measure of the stature of the fullness of Christ."

Peter Drucker records that "General Robert E. Lee did not appoint his generals on the basis of the absence of every weakness. He appointed them on the basis that each one appointed had one area of real strength ... Lee's men were 'single-purpose tools,' men of narrow but very great strength ... (The leader) who is concerned with what a man *cannot do* rather than what he *can do*, and who therefore tries to avoid weakness rather than make strength effective is a weak man himself. He probably sees strength in others as a threat to himself."

If a church, ministry or business is to grow exponentially there must be reasoned, thoughtful delegation. It is likely that no follower will "do the job" exactly like you would but if you do not delegate, the work cannot grow beyond a limited point. You can only do so much. Delegation opens up the possibility of unlimited expansion.

It may wound the pride to discover that the one to whom the task was delegated found "a better way" but the wise leader applauds the improvement and gladly adopts it for the good of the cause.

The leader *should not delegate*:

1. Responsibility to correct or discipline. Such an abdication looks like cowardice. In addition, we must remember that no one but the leader can discipline with the heart of the leader. Failure to have the heart of the leader intimately involved and reflected in situations of correction or discipline often leads to over-discipline and harsh treatment which embitters and alienates the follower.

2. A major problem.

3. Tasks that involve confidential information.

4. Responsibility to create and maintain morale.

Leadership Does Not ... Hire "Climbers" As Staff Members

—⚍—

Turf expanders and lobbyists who are not willing to subordinate their vision to the vision of the leader are potentially divisive. If an individual is not willing to implement the goals and philosophies of the leader he will be forever "writing his own ticket." The Apostle John wrote about such a situation in III John 9, 10, "I wrote unto the church: but Diotrephes, who loveth to have the preeminence among them, receiveth us not. Wherefore, if I come, I will remember his deeds which he doeth, prating against us with malicious words: and not content therewith, neither doth he himself receive the brethren, and forbiddeth them that would, and casteth them out of the church."

Beware of the staff member who stubbornly clings to his own "ticket." Watch out for the staff member who is a veritable free lancer who insists on creating his own "good ol' boy" network of pals and buddies, the fellow who is constantly ingratiating other followers or collecting I.O.U.s "signed by" members of the constituency!

If we want a Machiavelli type operative on our staff, then we should hire him! If we don't, we had better be careful when we are considering a potential staff member.

Paul wrote the following of Timothy, "But I trust in the Lord Jesus to send Timotheus shortly unto you, that I also may be of good comfort, when I know your state. For I have no man likeminded, who will naturally care for your state. For all seek their own, not the things which are Jesus Christ's. But ye know the proof of him, that, as a son with the father, he hath served with me in the gospel" (Philippians 2:19-22).

Leaders should never hire staff members who have independent ambitions and will not be satisfied to be an extension of the leader's emphasis and goals. Leaders should hire staff members who are content and happy to be team players. It is not ethical for a staff member to try to change the leader or the direction of a ministry *after* he has joined the team. Staff members who begin to make a habit of "second-guessing" or "knowing better" than the leader or listening sympathetically to criticism about the leader should be ethical enough to move elsewhere or be prepared to be dismissed. For an example of the kind of staff member a leader should not hire, read the story of David and Absalom found in II Samuel 15:2-6.

Leadership Does Not ... Fail To See That Details Are Cared For

—w—

In II Timothy 4:13 the aged apostle Paul gives a directive about details: The cloke, the books and the parchments. "The cloke that I left at Troas with Carpus, when thou comest, bring with thee, and the books, but especially the parchments."

General George S. Patton observed, "Issuing an order is worth about 10 percent. The remaining 90 percent consists of assuring proper and vigorous execution of the order."

The Confederate States of America's troops at Harper's Ferry were an untrained, undisciplined rabble when Stonewall Jackson was given command there. Within a matter of weeks a totally different atmosphere pervaded.

Captain John B. Imboden saw the great change in the short period of time and remarked, "The presence of a mastermind was visible in the changed condition of the camp. Perfect order reigned everywhere. Instruction in the *details* of military *duties* occupied Jackson's whole time. He urged the officers to call upon him for information about even the minutest details of duty."

Leadership Does Not ... Immediately Accept Second-Hand Reports

—⁂—

Leadership does not accept second-hand reports of discontent without requiring the names of primary sources.

"At the mouth of two witnesses, or three witnesses, shall he that is worthy of death be put to death; but at the mouth of one witness he shall not be put to death" (Deuteronomy 17:6).

Leadership does not assume that the problem or discontent is as serious as the "for-your-own-good" informant says. Informants are sometimes Absaloms who gain power and self-importance by playing both ends against the middle. In such cases one will notice that the informant thrives on mystery, intrigue and grape vines! The leader must, at all costs, avoid the paranoia trap into which the informant would either innocently or deliberately lead him. Proverbs 24:2 says, "For their heart studieth destruction, and their lips talk of mischief."

Some followers get their security in life from living in "the crisis mentality." They thrive on it. It makes them feel needed and important. It is an ego re-enforcer for them.

It's their adrenaline fix. They are addicted to the "rush" of crises.

Leaders are not stampeded into a "crisis mentality" by the hasty reports of emotionally volatile persons.

"It is an honour for a man to cease from strife: but every fool will be meddling" (Proverbs 20:3). You may learn that the one bringing the report is more of a chronic problem, a "well-intentioned dragon," than the one being reported on.

Neither does leadership assume that there is nothing whatsoever to what the informant says. This is the opposite and equally dangerous reaction – the ostrich reaction. Satan has devices to cloud issues off of both ends of the dock. We need to be aware of "both ends." The apostle Paul said, " ... lest Satan should get an advantage of us: for we are not ignorant of his devices" (II Corinthians 2:11).

Leadership Does Not ...
Discipline In Anger

———〜〜〜———

"**B**ut now ye also put off all these, anger, wrath, malice, blasphemy, filthy communication out of your mouth" (Colossians 3:8).

We have already seen that the violation of this principle cost General Patton dearly.

Bob Jones, Sr. (1883 - 1968)

Bobby Jones was born, the son of a sharecropper in Skipperville, Alabama – the second last of 12 children. "Dr. Bob" was born again when he was 11, started preaching when he was 13 and licensed to preach when he was 15. Before long he was preaching around the globe. By the time he was 40 he had preached 12,000 sermons to over 15 million people. In 1927 Dr. Jones founded the school which became Bob Jones University. Today students enroll from the United States and 34 foreign countries. The evangelist's last words were, "Mary Gaston, get my shoes. I must go to preach."

Leadership Does Not ... Discipline Without All The Facts

—ɯ—

"He that answereth a matter before he heareth it, it is folly and shame unto him" (Proverbs 18:13).

On one occasion Dr. Bob Jones, Sr. disciplined a young man who was a student at Bob Jones University. Later the world-famous evangelist learned that there were some mitigating factors of which he had not originally been aware.

He concluded that he had "been too hard on the boy," enquired as to his whereabouts and found him doing his laundry. Bob Jones, Sr. proceeded to apologize to the young man, encouraged him in his studies ... and gave him the money to wash and dry his clothes.

This anecdote should not lessen our regard for Dr. Jones. His sense of fairness and justice which led him to correct the situation was one of the character qualities that endeared him to thousands around the world.

Charles Haddon Spurgeon (1834 - 1892)

The "Prince of Preachers" was raised in Stambourne, England, by his grandfather, James, who was the pastor of the local Independent Church. He immersed himself in the Puritan collection in the parsonage library. By the time he was 15 he had become the boy-pastor of the Waterbeach Chapel in Teversham. In February, 1854, at 19, Spurgeon began his ministry at the New Park Street Chapel in London. Soon he had to ask his members to stay home during the evening service so others could attend. In his 39 years in London he baptized over 10,000 persons, preached to 10 million people and wrote the greatest body of Gospel literature by any one author in the English speaking world.

Leadership Does Not ... Fall Prey To The "Convoy Mentality"

—◊◊◊—

L eadership does not fall prey to the "convoy mentality" which says, "We cannot act until we have 100% agreement." You will seldom act if you always wait for 100 % agreement.

"But when Sanballat the Horonite, and Tobiah the servant, the Ammonite, and Geshem the Arabian, heard it, they laughed us to scorn, and despised us, and said, What is this thing that ye do? Will ye rebel against the king? Then answered I them, and said unto them, The God of heaven, he will prosper us; therefore we his servants will arise and build: but ye have no portion, nor right, nor memorial, in Jerusalem" (Nehemiah 2:19,20).

"He that observeth the wind shall not sow; and he that regardeth the clouds shall not reap" (Ecclesiastes 11:4).

Sixty church members refused to follow Charles Haddon Spurgeon from the disintegrating New Park Street Chapel building to the new Metropolitan Tabernacle. That refusal is the last that was ever heard of them.

Any vote above an 85% affirmative vote is a good vote for a leader who is implementing change. Thank God for it and get on with the implementation of the change – before the 15% have time to lobby for "rethinking" the matter.

Votes under 75% affirmative may suggest the need to clarify or correct misconceptions before you proceed.

The most secure kind of leadership is leadership by strong consensus. But most of the decisions that have impacted human history for good have not been decisions born out of a complete consensus. It is an insecure and proud leader who must have 100% agreement all of the time. Minority disagreement can be thought-provoking and serve as a "check and balance."

We do, however, need to require that the minority graciously accept the majority vote in the name of both Christian and democratic principles. Those who keep lobbying on behalf of the "lost, minority position" should be asked to desist or implement their minority view elsewhere.

The convoy mentality paralyzes.

The convoy mentality will always lead to inertia. Inertia is deadly. It is easier to keep an object moving than it is to start it from a standstill.

Leadership Does Not …
Assume Itself
To Be Irreplaceable

—∿—

We are told in Romans 12:3, "For I say, through the grace given unto me, to every man that is among you, not to think of himself more highly than he ought to think; but to think soberly, according as God hath dealt to every man the measure of faith."

Major General William F. Ward said, "People who win great battles … have a vision of what's required for victory, and they find a realistic way of making that vision come true … They detach themselves, take a very cold look, almost as if they might be dead tomorrow."

Leadership remembers its mortality and dispensability.

A healthy sense of dispensability engenders courage and dispels fear. It leads to the heroism born of abandonment.

On The Vanity of Earthly Greatness

The tusks that clashed in nightly brawls
Of mastadons, are billiard balls.
The sword of Charlemagne the Just
Is ferric oxide, known as rust.

The grizzly bear whose potent hug
Was feared by all, is now a rug.
Great Caesar's bust is on the shelf,
And I don't feel so well myself.

- Arthur Guiterman

Jonathan Edwards wrote, "The bodies of those that made such a noise and tumult when alive, when dead, lie as quietly among the graves of their neighbors as any others."

"Charlemagne gave instructions that when he died he should be buried seated in the royal posture of a ruling monarch on a throne. Then he directed that the Gospels should be laid on his knees, his sword beside him, the imperial crown on his head, and the royal mantle on his shoulders. And thus his body remained for 180 years.

"About 1000 A.D. the tomb was opened by the Emperor Otho. They found the skeleton of Charlemagne, dissolved and dismembered into various hideous postures. The skull was still wearing the crown. The bony finger of the skeleton was pointing to the verse of Scripture, 'For what is a man profited, if he shall gain the whole world, and lose his own soul?' (Matthew 16:26).

"The various relics were collected and used in the coronation of the emperors of Germany to signify their greatness and succession from Charlemagne."
– Massie

Arthur M. Schlesinger said, "Leaders are not demigods; they put on their trousers one leg after another just like ordinary mortals. No leader is infallible, and every leader needs to be reminded of this at regular intervals. Irreverence irritates leaders but is their salvation. Unquestioning submission corrupts leaders and demeans followers. Making a cult of a leader is always a mistake."

At the climax of the Battle of Waterloo when it became obvious that the British were going to win, one of Wellington's men called to him and said, "We are getting into enclosed ground, and your life is too valuable to be thrown away."

Wellington replied, "Never mind. Let them fire away. The battle's won; my life is of no consequence now."

Leaders abandon it all – for the sake of the call.

Leadership Does Not ...
Threaten To Resign

—⟋⟍—

"**B**e not rash with thy mouth, and let not thine heart be hasty to utter any thing before God: for God is in heaven, and thou upon earth: therefore let they words be few. For a dream cometh through the multitude of business; and a fool's voice is known by multitude of words. When thou vowest a vow unto God, defer not to pay it, for he hath no pleasure in fools: pay that which thou has vowed. Better is it that thou shouldest not vow, than that thou shouldest vow and not pay. Suffer not thy mouth to cause thy flesh to sin; neither say thou before the angel, that it was an error: wherefore should God be angry at thy voice, and destroy the work of thine hand: For in the multitude of dreams and many words there are also divers vanities: but fear thou God" (Ecclesiastes 5:2-7).

Even if you threaten to resign just one time and fail to follow through with it, you have permanently wounded your credibility with all who hear about it. They will be quick to conclude, even if unfairly or untruly, that you used the threat as a tool to manipulate and get your own way. They will conclude that you value your own agenda more than their security. Followers eventually distrust and resent leaders who use their followers' sense of security as a pawn or bargaining chip to further their own ends.

Most people know that the threat of resignation ratchets up the "stakes" or consequences in any conflict and intuitively view this tactic as a "low blow" not worthy of Christian interaction.

Someone has well said that "quitting is usually a long-term solution to a short-term problem."

Lee Roberson (1909 -)

Dr. Lee Roberson was born in English, Indiana. In 1911 his family moved to Louisville. At the age of 14 he heard Mrs. Daisy Hawes explain the plan of salvation. He trusted Christ and made his public profession of faith. He became staff soloist at radio station WHAS while attending university. In 1942, after 5 years in evangelism, he became the pastor of the Highland Park Baptist Church in Chattanooga, Tennessee. His 41-year pastorate saw 61,000 baptisms. In 1946 he started Tennessee Temple University. He continued as President until 1974 when he became Chancellor. TTU has graduated over 12,000 students.

Leadership Does Not ...
Become Over-Familiar
With Followship

—⟲⟲—

L eadership does not become over-familiar. It does not create a "buddy-buddy" relationship with followers. "Yea, mine own familiar friend, in whom I trusted, which did eat of my bread, hath lifted up his heel against me ... For it was not an enemy that reproached me, then I could have borne it: neither was it he that hated me that did magnify himself against me; then I would have hid myself from him: But it was thou, a man mine equal, my guide, and mine acquaintance. We took sweet counsel together, and walked unto the house of God in company" (Psalm 41:9 and 55:12-14).

The over-familiar leader is the over-exposed leader. Over-familiarity evaporates the buffer zone of mystery which should guard any relationship that matters.

Dr. Lee Roberson was a master of the delicate balance between the wisdom of accessibility and the wisdom of inaccessibility.

Only fools "let it all hang out."

Stonewall Jackson said, "It is not desirable to have a large number of intimate friends; you may have many acquaintances, but few intimate friends."

William Hazlett said, "Though familiarity may not breed contempt, it takes off the edge of admiration." Edward Gibbon wrote, "Conversation enriches the understanding, but solitude is the school of genius."

Whenever Michelangelo, that "divine madman," as Richardson once wrote on the back of one of his drawings, was meditating on some great design, he closed himself up from the world. "Why do you lead such a solitary life?" asked a friend. "Art," replied the sublime artist, "is a jealous god; it requires the whole and entire man." During his mighty labor in the Sistine Chapel he refused to have any communication with any person, even at his own house.

In his book, *Paul the Leader*, J. Oswald Sanders acknowledges that General Charles de Gaulle and "many other great men" practiced "the greatness of isolation."

George Washington advised, "Be courteous to all, but intimate with few, and let those few be well tried before you give them your confidence."

Regarding Jonathan Edwards, Iain H. Murray writes, "From the outset it was not Jonathan Edwards' custom to pull up his horse and pass the time of day with his many parishioners ... He lived somewhat apart."

Wess Roberts, Ph.D., who wrote the *New York Times* bestseller for business leaders, *Leadership Secrets of Attila the Hun,* said, "Chieftains who drink with their Huns become one with them and are no longer their chieftain."

H. Essame wrote, "General Patton, like Pershing and Wellington, maintained his distance from the main body of his staff and lived apart with his command group." Some business leaders call this *the paretto principle*. This is precisely what Jesus practiced. There were the "multitudes," the "twelve" and the "three." It was not a matter of playing favorites. It was a matter of different degrees of concentrated training and mentoring. Jesus was usually accessible but He also had a buffer zone when the situation demanded it.

Alexander Whyte, the celebrated Scottish preacher, wrote, "Your people will not care one straw what you say from the pulpit if you sup heartily with them afterward." John Bunyan said that many a sermon is lost in the "fellowship" of the Sunday dinner which takes place after. G. Campbell Morgan spoke about more prophets being ruined by eating out with followers than in any other way.

Charles G. Finney said, "Do not make the impression that you're fond of good dinners and like to be invited out to dine with followers. It'll be a snare to you and a stumbling block to them."

In *Threescore And Ten* Vance Havner wrote, "Do not accept gifts that make you beholden to the giver. A free trip to the Holy Land can bind a minister more securely than Delilah tied up Samson. Do not dwell in your ivory tower and neglect the flock, but do not become so involved with your flock that you cannot be a prophet on Sunday. I have seen good men become the flunkeys and bellhops of their congregation ... Do not make cronies of any of your flock *for your buddy may turn out to be your biggest problem* ... Do not talk your views, preach them. If you are always talking your views in social conversation, you'll have nothing left to say in the pulpit. Dr. John H. Jowett expressed himself from the pulpit but had little to say in general conversation."

Well-renown preacher Charles Simeon said, "I compare myself to a bottle of carbonated beverage: with the lid or stopper on and opened only twice a week, I make a good report; but if I were opened every day, I should soon be as (diluted and insipid) as ditch water." Question: who is attracted very long to ditch water?!

W. Steven Brown, President of the Fortune Group, makes the following comment, "So often managers want to be the employees' buddy after hours, then come into the office and manage them tomorrow - and the employees will not allow it. It is an either-or situation. You must be the buddy *or* the manager. Successful hybrids do not exist in such a situation."

In his book, *I Rode With Stonewall*, Henry Kyd Douglas wrote, "After dinner General Stonewall Jackson returned to his room, and I saw him no more that day. The General always kept himself very much apart and, although he was uniformly polite to all persons who came to see him, he did not encourage social calls."

No leader can afford to over-socialize, horse around, kabbitz or get overly familiar. Getting "too close" has ruined thousands of leaders.

In an interview in the *Biblical Evangelist*, March 1, 1990, Mrs. John R. Rice said, "Dr. Rice liked to be with his family, and he kept us very close to himself. He didn't go out to eat with the fellows; in fact, we didn't go out to eat with people much since we took our children wherever we went. He would rather be home than anywhere."

Dr. C.I. Scofield said, "Before God uses a man greatly, He isolates him. He gives him *a separating experience* ... And when this separating experience is over, those about the person God is going to greatly use are no less loved than before but they are no longer depended upon. The individual realizes that he is separated unto God, that the wings of his soul have learned to beat the upper air, and that God has shown him unspeakable things. If we mount up with wings as eagles, we must count upon some experience of misunderstanding ... We can avoid this. We can nest low enough to be understood by the carnal ... but if we take the upper air, we must, like the eagle, go alone ... Christ will never be satisfied until He has each of us separated unto Himself."

Napoleon actually became a friend to his soldiers and gave them gifts such as tobacco. This was unusual for a general, but it earned him the loyalty and devotion of his men. However, this friendship was not without its element of isolation or aloofness.

In Will Durant's *Age of Napoleon*, the young Napoleon says, "Always alone in the midst of men, I come to my room to dream by myself, to abandon myself to my melancholy in all its sharpness."

Another leader said, "Around us there is continual movement. People talking, newspapers, radio and TV. With the discipline and moderation of leaders we must say, 'Beyond certain limits you do not exist for me. I am a (pastor) of the Lord. I must have a little silence for my soul. I distance myself from you to be with my God for awhile.'"

A few days after Eisenhower became President, General O.N. Bradley, who had for forty years always called him "Ike," addressed him as "Mr. President." Eisenhower recorded his feelings, "General Bradley's salutation put me on notice ... I would to a very definite degree be separated from all others, including my oldest friends."

Leadership Does Not … Lose Its Sense Of Right And Wrong

—ɯ—

Leadership retains a strong perception of "moral ought."

"And not rather, (as we be slanderously reported, and as some affirm that we say,) Let us do evil, that good may come? whose damnation is just" (Romans 3:8).

General Robert E. Lee was motivated by the conviction that "duty is the most beautiful word in the English language." He said, "There is a true glory and a true honor; the glory of duty done." Is it any wonder that a man with such a conviction could "lose the War between the States" and ride away the most highly respected general of all? Lee was lauded for his consistency, his devotion to duty, "never abandoned to personal emotion."

After he was sworn in as President at the U.S. capitol in 1953, Dwight Eisenhower prayed, "Give us, we pray, the power to discern clearly right from wrong, and allow all our words and actions to be governed thereby."

In *The Secret Life of Bill Clinton: The Unreported Stories*, Ambrose Evans-Pritchard wrote, "The American Elite, I am afraid to say, is almost beyond redemption. Moral relativism has set in so deeply that the gilded classes have become incapable of discerning right from wrong. Everything can be explained away, especially by journalists. Life is one great moral mush – sophistry washed down with Chardonnay."[18]

Abraham Lincoln said, "I am not bound to win, but I am bound to be true. I am not bound to succeed, but I am bound to live by the light I have."

The leader who has no sense of duty or "ought" is an ethical zero. He will reproduce followers who do not know how to be loyal.

A 13-year-old, Mexican girl was found taking care of her abandoned brothers and sisters. The girl was questioned as to the circumstances. In the course of the questioning someone said, "No one told you that you had to take care of your brothers and sisters." "What about the voice inside me?" replied the girl.

Stonewall Jackson said, "Through life let your principle object be the discharge of duty … Resolve to perform what you ought; perform without fail what you resolve … Sacrifice your life rather than your word."

Solon (630-560 B.C.) said, "He who has learned to obey will know how to command."

Charles H. Spurgeon said, "Learn to say no; it will be more use to you than to be able to read Latin."

Of the Duke of Wellington, it was said that "the principle on which (he) always acted was his own undeviating ideal of duty."

Dr. Clarence Sexton, Pastor of the Temple Baptist Church and President of Crown College in Powell, Tennessee, wrote, "We have moved from the violation of God's standards to the repudiation of God's standards to the popularization and glorification of evil."[19]

May God in His mercy grant us a revival and send us a new generation of leaders who have a strong sense of right and wrong and lead by the compulsions of a "moral ought."

Leadership Does Not ... Fail To Seize The Moment Of Opportunity

—∽—

"Do thy diligence to come shortly unto me ... Do thy diligence to come before winter" (II Timothy 2:9, 21).

In Act 4, Scene 3 of *Julius Caesar*, William Shakespeare puts the following words in the mouth of Cassius:

> There is a tide in the affairs of men,
> Which, taken at the flood, leads on to fortune;
> Omitted, all the voyage of their life
> Is bound in shallows and in miseries.

Author Allen Tate and many other strategists believe that the South would have won the Civil War had the Confederates marched on Washington immediately after their victory at Manassas on July 21, 1861. The Confederate President, Jefferson Davis, chose to do nothing.

An Arabian proverb says, "Four things come not back: the sped arrow, the spoken word, time past and the neglected opportunity."

In *The Four Quartets* T.S. Elliot wrote,

> Footfalls echo in the memory,
> Down the passage we did not take
> Towards the door we never opened
> Into the rose garden.

Victor Kiam of the Remington Company said, "Procrastination is opportunity's natural assassin."

Napoleon had a veritable passion for always being on time. His motto was, "Time is everything," and he once said, "I may lose battles, but no one will ever see me lose minutes."

General Douglas MacArthur said that in war, all disasters can be explained by two words, "Too late."

John Bowers described Stonewall Jackson in the following way, "He knew what he had to do. He acted. His military plans were simple and direct ... strokes of genius ... in the midst of chaos, he snatched the reins of the beast while others pondered. He forged into the unknown."

Andrew S. Grove, the Chairman of Intel, said, "There is at least one point in the history of any company where you have to change dramatically to rise to the next performance level. Miss that moment, and you start to decline."

Leadership Does Not ...
Fail To Carefully
And Deliberately Choose Its Battles

—⁓—

66 **A**fter whom is the king of Israel come out? after whom dost thou pursue: after a dead dog, after a flea" (I Samuel 24:14). In I Kings 22:3, 29-37, we read of two kings deciding whether to go to battle or not. They unwisely decided to go to battle against the advice of the Lord's prophet. They not only lost the battle, one of them was killed.

On October 7, 1862, William Joseph Hardee instructed Braxton Bragg as follows, "Don't scatter your forces. There is one rule in our profession that should never be forgotten – it is to throw the masses of your troops on the fractions of the enemy."

Leaders win by exercising the art of selective warfare. They know when and where to fight. Victories come as the result of focusing time and energy on wisely selected battles. Being drawn into too many battles on too many fronts invites defeat.

The Don Quixote complex of trying to ride your horse in all directions at the same time looks ludicrous and soon wears out both horse and rider!

Battlefields, arenas of war, come into being when a general decides, "Here I'll stand."

Regarding the Korean War General Omar Bradley said, "(We are fighting) the wrong war, at the wrong place, at the wrong time and with the wrong enemy."

Simplify your leadership by reducing your cause or mission to a set of convictions or non-negotiables. Fight for these – not your preferences.

Isaac was provoked, no doubt, when the herdsmen of Gerar repeatedly claimed the wells that had been dug by Isaac's own men. The aggravation was such that Isaac named the wells "Esek," which means "contention," and "Sitnah," which means "enmity" (Genesis 26:19-22).

However, Isaac wisely decided that on this occasion the choice to fight would rise more out of a wounded pride than of long-range consequence. He thus opted to simply remove himself and his cause from the environment of provocation.

One insecure and chest-thumping pastor said, "I just love a good fight." Successful leaders fight as a last resort. There will be enough fights in the course of one's time without looking for one.

General George Patton said, "Never fight a fight when nothing is accomplished by the victory."

To fail to fight when principle is at stake is cowardly appeasement. To fight when principle is not at stake is ego. And ego has destroyed more leaders than any other single thing!

Never seek a fight but never yield a conflict where the glory of God would be jeopardized by the yielding.

In his State of the Union address in 2006, President George W. Bush said, "Retreat is not peace; retreat is not honor."

Dwight D. Eisenhower said, "What counts is not necessarily the size of the dog in the fight; it's the size of the fight in the dog."

Robert E. Lee (1807 - 1870)

Robert E. Lee was born near Montross, Virginia. He was raised to have a deep devotion to his native state. In 1825 he entered West Point. When the Civil War began in 1861, though he did not support slavery, he cast his lot with his beloved Virginia. His fame rests on his military achievements as Supreme Commander against overwhelming odds and on his sterling personal character. He was never known to smoke, drink alcoholic beverages or use profanity. Ulysses S. Grant, to whom Lee finally surrendered, said, "There was not a man in the Confederacy whose influence with the whole people was as great as his."

Leadership Does Not …
Fail To Realize
That Sometimes We Must Lose
A Battle

—ɱ—

L eadership does not fail to realize that sometimes we must lose a battle in order to win the overall war. (We speak here of tactical, procedural matters – not matters of essential doctrine.)

"We are troubled on every side, yet not distressed; we are perplexed, but not in despair; Persecuted, but not forsaken; cast down, but not destroyed; Always bearing about in the body the dying of the Lord Jesus, that the life also of Jesus might be made manifest in our body. For we which live are always delivered unto death for Jesus' sake, that the life also of Jesus might be made manifest in our mortal flesh" (II Corinthians 4:8-11).

Both General Robert E. Lee and the famous Swamp Fox, Francis Marion, almost always knew when to give now in order to be in a position to take later.

There seems to have been one tragic exception in the career of Robert E. Lee. Most admirers of Lee reluctantly agree that this is what Lee failed to realize at Gettysburg. Lee persisted though his men were being mowed down like so many stalks of wheat. 28,000 Confederate soldiers died. 38 Confederate battle flags were left behind. Union officers tied them behind their horses and dragged them in the dust to taunt the fleeing southerners. When he finally gave the command to retreat, surveyed the casualties on the field and watched the survivors limping and crawling off the field, Lee lowered his head towards his chest and said, "It's all my fault." He wrote Jefferson Davis, President of the Confederacy, and offered to resign.

William Wilberforce spent his entire political career trying to abolish the slave trade. The British Parliament voted to do so two days before his death! In his biography of Wilberforce, David J. Vaughan writes, "Losing to win means you compromise in tactic but not in principle. It is better to attain a partial victory than to suffer a total defeat. Principles must be implemented with prudence."[20]

The Duke of Wellington said that the best test of a general is "to know when to retreat, and how to do it." He is a coward who always retreats, and he is a fool who never retreats.

Macaulay described Alexander the Great as one who was "often defeated in battle, always successful in war."

Benjamin Disraeli, Queen Victoria's "preferred" Prime Minister said, "Next to knowing when to seize an opportunity, the most important thing in life is to know when to forego an advantage."

Leadership Does Not ... Play Games With The Truth

—⁓—

"**M**ercy and truth preserve the king: and his throne is upholden by mercy ... Buy the truth, and sell it not; also wisdom, and instruction, and understanding" (Proverbs 20:28 and 23:23).

"And ye shall know the truth, and the truth shall make you free" (John 8:32).

Picasso would walk around muttering, "Truth cannot exist ... truth does not exist ... I am God. I am God." Françoise Gilot was one of his wives and mistresses. In her book, *My Life With Picasso*, she wrote, "Picasso was like a conqueror marching through life, accumulating power, women, wealth, glory, but none of that was very satisfying anymore."[21]

When he was defending how President Lyndon Johnson conducted the Vietnam War, George McBundy wrote, "Grey is the color of truth."

Peggy Noonan wrote in *The Case Against Hillary Clinton*, published in 2000, "With Mrs. Hillary Clinton reporters seem to limit the number of quotes they use. They tend to concentrate instead on the venue of the speech, the atmospherics surrounding it, and pictures of the event.

"There's a reason for this.

"Almost a year into her candidacy (for Senator) I gathered as many Hillary speech quotes as I could and reviewed them. They are relentlessly banal. Why would a dramatic candidate for high public office make it a point, every day, to say nothing that would be the least bit memorable or interesting to potential voters?

"Because she has a strategy. The strategy is to use words not to pierce through the fog of voices and sounds in which we all live, but to add to the fog. She is using words not to reveal but to conceal, not to make clear but to confuse. She is not trying to communicate her thoughts, ideas, and plans; she is merely trying to communicate an impression with pictures.

"For as long as she can in the campaign, she will limit her communication to the symbolic.

"There is another reason she says nothing interesting in public. It is that if she declares, or allows herself to be drawn out about, her real philosophy and views, she enters a danger area … She will continue to say nothing because she wants not to explain her stands but to obscure them."

One of John F. Kennedy's biographers said that Kennedy was a manipulator, a master of "using candor in lieu of truth." People thought he had told them the truth. But, in reality, he had told them nothing of true importance. The smarmy, homey "candid" moments set people up for the big lie.[21]

Leadership Does Not ...
Over-Regulate

—w—

L eadership is resisting the temptation to over-regulate. (And, yes, this is a *good* rule!)

"Think not that I am come to destroy the law, or the prophets: I am not come to destroy, but to fulfill ... For they bind heavy burdens and grievous to be borne, and lay them on men's shoulders; but they themselves will not move them with one of their fingers. But all their works they do for to be seen of men: they make broad their phylacteries, and enlarge the borders of their garments" (Matthew 5:17 and 23:4, 5).

"Ye are my friends, if ye do whatsoever I command you" (John 15:14).

"Who also hath made us able ministers of the new testament, not of the letter, but of the spirit: for the letter killeth, but the spirit giveth life" (II Corinthians 3:6).

"For this is the love of God, that we keep his commandments: and his commandments are not grievous" (I John 5:3).

Homes, schools, colleges, universities, corporations and nations need rules. Without basic rules chaos would reign. We are all still depraved. Most rules in churches and Christian organizations are in place because someone back there somewhere abused Christian liberty.

Even Massachusetts Institute of Technology and Harvard psychology professor Steven Pinker confesses to being shaken by an experience from his teenage years which undermined his "authority not needed" hypothesis. He makes this confession in his book *The Blank Slate*, where he writes:

"As a young teenager in a proudly peaceable Canada during the romantic 1960s, I was a true believer in Bakunin's anarchism. I laughed off my parents' argument that if the government ever laid down its arms all hell would break loose. Our competing predictions were put to the test at 8:00 A.M. on October 17, 1969, when the Montreal police went on strike. By 11:20 A.M. the first bank was robbed. By noon most downtown stores had closed because of looting. Within a few more hours, taxi drivers burned down the garage of a limousine service that competed with them for airport customers, a rooftop sniper killed a provincial police officer, rioters broke into several hotels and restaurants, and a doctor slew a burglar in his suburban home. By the end of the day, six banks had been robbed, a hundred shops had been looted, twelve fires had been set, forty carloads of storefront glass had been broken, and three million dollars in property damage had been inflicted, before city authorities had to call in the army and, of course, the Mounties to restore order. This decisive empirical test left my politics in tatters."

Every organization among men has to have checks on depravity. Dr. Pinker saw firsthand what happens when all restraints are removed.

However, we must remember what Pastor Ken Endean wrote several years ago in an article in *Today's Christian Preacher*. He said, "Rules without relationship equal rebellion."

The account of the Pharisees' reaction to the disciples rubbing a few heads of cereal grain in their hands on the Sabbath in Luke 6:1-5 is an illustration of what happens when you have rules without relationship. Our Lord defended his hungry disciples because the issue was not the moral Law of God. Jesus was never ashamed to declare that he had come "not to destroy but to fulfill" the moral Law of God (Matthew 5:17).

The issue was the ceremonial laws which had been added by men. G. Campbell Morgan writes, "Jesus was constantly protesting against adding human tradition to the law ... When (the order of Pharisees) sprang up ... it was a mighty movement. But gradually, in the process of the intervening years, these men ... began interpreting the law; and in order to guard it, they superimposed upon it interpretations and applications of it."

On the Sabbath issue the Great Synagogue had given 39 prohibitions which were subsequently divided into six minor categories under each of these 39 prohibitions! The prohibitions were the "abhoth." The minor categories were the "toldoth" or "descendants" of the prohibitions. The end result was that there were 234 prohibitions from one Law!

Frederic Louis Godet wrote, "It is an error to regard (Jesus) as having, under certain circumstances, set aside the law of the Sabbath … He only transgressed the arbitrary enactments with which Pharisaism had surrounded it."

Tacitus, the Roman historian, said, "The more corrupt the state, the more numerous the laws."

When Robert E. Lee became president of Washington College he said, "We have only one rule here – to act like a gentleman at all times." Lee also said, "The real honest man is honest from conviction of what is right, not from policy."

Calvin Miller said, "Rules blunt the appetite for Christ. Joy intrigues."

Roy B. Zuck said, "I read in a USA publication in 1998 that the USA had at that time on the books 35 million laws to interpret and enforce the 10 Commandments."

You may have read this compilation of just a few of our profound laws:

In Alaska, it is illegal to push a live moose out of a moving airplane.

In Connecticut, you can be stopped by the police for biking over 65 miles per hour. You are not allowed to walk across a street on your hands.

In Florida, women may be fined for falling asleep under a hair dryer, as can the salon owner. Unmarried women are prohibited from parachuting on Sunday. If an elephant is left tied to a parking meter, the parking fee has to be paid just as it would for a vehicle.

In Indiana, bathing is prohibited during the winter. Citizens are not allowed to ride in a public streetcar within four hours of eating garlic.

In Iowa, kisses may last for as long as, but no more than, five minutes.

In Kentucky, it is illegal to transport an ice cream cone in your pocket.

In Louisiana, biting someone with your natural teeth is "simple assault," while biting someone with your false teeth is "aggravated assault."

In Massachusetts, mourners at a wake may not eat more than three sandwiches. Snoring is prohibited unless all bedroom windows are closed and securely locked.

A Vancouver city law requires all motor vehicles to carry anchors as emergency brakes.

A San Francisco ordinance forbids the reuse of confetti.

In Danville, Pennsylvania, fire hydrants must be checked one hour before all fires.

In Seattle, it is illegal to carry a concealed weapon of more than six feet in length.

An Oklahoma law states that a driver of any vehicle involved in an accident resulting in death shall immediately stop ... and give his name and address to the person struck.

In Lakefield, Ontario, a piece of noise-abatement legislation was passed which permits birds to sing for thirty minutes during the day and fifteen minutes at night.

In the April 14, 1996, *Hammond Times*, columnist Phil Wieland reported that a recent state law in Texas requires criminals to give victims 24 hours notice of any intended crime. Another Texas law makes it illegal to milk another person's cow. It is illegal to fish in one's pajamas in Chicago. Another law in the state of Illinois declares that it is illegal to mispronounce the name "Joliet." In Gary, Indiana, it is illegal to attend the theater within four hours of eating garlic.

Now, aren't you proud of our brilliant jurisprudence?!

A cartoon by Doug Hall in the Winter 1993 issue of *Leadership Magazine* showed a pastor with a pointer standing in front of a blackboard crammed with writing under the heading "Ivy Hill Church Membership Class." The caption read, "Some churches use the acronym 'TULIP' to remember their beliefs. We use 'CHRYSANTHEMUM.'"

The "rule" of "law" can become downright ludicrous. Consider what some have called "the Case of the Burning Cigars."

A Charlotte, North Carolina, man, having just purchased a case of very rare, expensive cigars, insured them against – get this – fire. Within a month, having smoked all 24 of these cigars, the man filed a claim against the insurance company. In his claim, the man stated that he had lost the cigars in a "series of small fires."

The insurance company refused to pay, citing the obvious reason that the man had consumed the cigars in a normal fashion. The man sued and won.

In delivering the ruling, the judge stated that the man held a policy from the company in which it had warranted that the cigars were insurable, and also guaranteed that it would insure the cigars against fire, without defining what it considered unacceptable fire. It was obligated therefore to compensate the insured for his loss.

Rather than enduring a lengthy and costly appeals process, the insurance company accepted the judge's ruling and paid the man $15,000 for the rare cigars he lost in the "fires." After the man cashed his check, however, the insurance company had him arrested – on 24 counts of arson.

With his own insurance claim as testimony from the previous case being used as evidence against him, the man was convicted of intentionally burning the rare cigars and sentenced to a year in jail!

In his address to the military on October 11, 1798, President John Adams said, "We have no government armed with power capable of contending with human passions unbridled by morality and religion. Avarice, ambition, revenge or gallantry would break the strongest cords of our Constitution as a whale goes through a net. Our Constitution was made only for a moral and religious people. It is wholly inadequate to the government of any other."

Benjamin Franklin said, "Let me add that only a virtuous people are capable of freedom. As nations become more corrupt and vicious, they have more need of masters."

Dr. Bob Jones, Sr. said, "A *don't* religion is not enough. The way to keep from *don'ting* is to *do* so much that you don't have time to *don't*."

A Greek proverb says, "Things forbidden have a secret charm."

Charles Haddon Spurgeon said, "The more rules there are, the more I want to break them."

Proverbs 9:17 reads, "Stolen waters are sweet, and bread eaten in secret [surreptitiously] is pleasant." Forbidden fruit is alluring.

Robert H. Bork wrote, "No ideal, however worthy, can be pressed forever without turning into something else, turning in fact into its opposite."[22]

What is Judge Bork saying? He is saying that we become what we fixate on. Lao-tzu (604 – 531 B.C.) said, "The greater the number of laws and enactments, the more thieves and robbers there will be."

Some years ago there was a hotel in Seattle, Washington, that was built right up to the pier. The management posted a sign inside the window of each room that faced the pier. The sign read, "No fishing from the hotel windows." Of course, that is precisely what many occupants of those rooms did anyway. A photographer took a picture one day when there were a good number of fishing poles hanging out the hotel windows and showed the picture to the hotel manager. The manager said, "The 'No Fishing' signs are not doing any good. We may as well take them down." The signs were removed. The fishing from the windows stopped! The signs had served as both a suggestion and an enticement.

René Descartes (1596 – 1650) wrote, "A state is better governed which has but few laws, and those laws strictly observed."

Benjamin Franklin wrote, "Laws too gentle are seldom obeyed; too severe, seldom executed." And Honoré de Balzac (1799 – 1850) said, "Laws are spider webs through which the big flies pass and the little ones get caught."

Jack Kemp, former Buffalo Bills football player and Vice Presidential candidate, said, "People obey the law for one of two reasons: they either love God or fear punishment. When both of these break down, the result is an environment that breeds violence, poverty and anarchy."

Some people confuse principles with rules. A principle is something that comes from inside a person. A rule is an outward restriction. To obey a principle, you have to use your mental and moral powers. To obey a rule you only have to do what the rule says. Dr. Frank Crane pointed out the difference neatly, "A rule supports us by the armpits over life's mountain passes. A principle makes us surefooted."

Commenting on the problem of sin and transgression, Christmas Evans said, "Life is the only cure for death. Not the prescriptions of duty, not the threats of punishment and damnation, not the arts and refinements of education, but new, spiritual, Divine Life."

George D. Watson said, "There are two great divisions among religious people; those who serve God legally, and those who serve Him lovingly."

Lao-tzu said, "The greatest administrators do not achieve production through constraints and limitations. They provide opportunities."

Winston Churchill said, "If you have 10,000 regulations, you destroy all respect for the law."

Ronald Reagan said, "I've been told that since the beginning of civilization, millions and millions of laws have not improved on the Ten Commandments one bit."

In *Leading with the Heart*, Coach Mike Krzyzewski of Duke University, award-winning college basketball coach, said the following:

"The fact that I *don't* have a hard and fast rule gives me flexibility in cases like these. It provides me the latitude to lead. It also allows me to show that I care about the kids on my team and it demonstrates that I'm trying to be fair-minded.

"Too many rules get in the way of leadership. They just put you in a box and, sooner or later, a rule-happy leader will wind up in the situation where he wants to use some discretion but is forced to go along with some decree that he himself has concocted. [Witness King Darius in Daniel chapter 6!]

"Of course, a few leaders like to be backed up by a long list of do's and don't's. 'OOPS, you did this on the list. I got'cha.' Well, I don't want to be a team of

'I gotchas.' I got'cha means 'I' rather than 'we.' And a leader who sets too many rules is making it appear that it is 'my' team, rather than 'our' team.

"The truth is that many people set rules to keep from making decisions. Not me. I don't want to be a manager or a dictator. I want to be a leader – and leadership is ongoing, adjustable, flexible, and dynamic. As such, leaders have to maintain a certain amount of discretion.

"At times, there may be extenuating circumstances for a person violating a rule."

A prime example is Jonathan's eating the honey when his father, King Saul, had made a rule against it (I Samuel 14)!

Robert E. Lee's diary contains long notations on child rearing. He emphasized the need "not only to make the child obey externally but *internally* to make the obedience sincere and hearty."

In the January, 1997, issue of *Balance*, a periodical for educators published by Bob Jones University, Dr. Jim Berg wrote,

We are not biblically successful in Christian education when we produce students who merely seem to stay out of trouble, who embrace our standards, or who 'just say no' to the worldliness around them. This kind of student may reflect a refreshing measure of character from a human standpoint, but his practice of a moral ideal or code of ethics is not necessarily Christlikeness. He can perhaps win many earthly awards with a measure of personal character developed by strong self-discipline (I Corinthians 9:23-24), but he can win the Lord's final approval only by reflecting the image of Christ. *Christian* character (Christlikeness) is formed only when the believer is continually "beholding [in the Word of God] the glory of the Lord." Only then is he "changed into the same image" by the Spirit of God, and our goal in Christian education is realized.

Dr. Berg has just described "Leadership ... and life ... by the Book!"

Meg Greenfield entitled her December 15, 1997, editorial in *Newsweek* magazine, "The Colin Powell Test." In what was surely viewed by many as a very politically incorrect commentary on affirmative action, she said, "There are some good purposes that require discretion, not codification, that will be better served by the slightly fuzzy mandate than one that is carved in stone in formal legalese."

In his book, *Be Ye Holy*, Dr. Fred Moritz writes, "Spirituality is not determined by outward conformity to a prescribed standard for human conduct, whether that standard is found in Scripture or set by man. But the believer who refuses to conform to the standards of Scripture will *always* reveal the glaring lack of a right attitude toward God and His holiness. When a believer, on the other hand, develops the proper perspective toward God and His holiness, he will gladly live in conformity to the standards which God sets in His Word. Those in places of leadership need to be sure that they stress the Christian's walk with God over the standards which they find it necessary to set and enforce."

The leader must *know* the rule and the reason for the rule and be prepared to explain the reason for the rule at any time. He must also be such a combination of integrity, ethical behavior, rectitude and grace that when he allows an exception to the rule, followers will know that there is a valid reason for the exception which exception only serves to strengthen and validate the general rule.

There are times when even the king-designate, David of Bethlehem himself, will need to eat a little "shewbread." Jesus approved of David's making an exception to the ceremonial law. (It was not a moral issue.) "Have ye not read so much as this, what David did, when himself was an hungred, and they which were with him; How he went into the house of God, and did take and eat the shewbread, and gave also to them that were with him; which it is not lawful to eat but for the priests alone? ... The Son of man is Lord also of the Sabbath" (Luke 6:3-5).

Come to think of it, I am a little hungry myself! "Leadership – by the Book" is no easy task.

Footnotes

—⁓ɯ⁓—

1. *The New Dictionary of Thoughts – A Cyclopedia of Quotations*; (Garden City, NY: Hanover House, 1852).

2. Stephen Abbott Northrop, *A Cloud of Witnesses*; (Portland, OR: Mantle Ministries, 1987).

3. Dorothy Davis, "Clarksburg Exponent," *Telegram*; (May 5, 1985).

4. James I. Robertson, Jr., *Stonewall Jackson, The Man, The Soldier, The Legend*; (Macmillan Publishing).

5. George Francis Henderson, *Stonewall Jackson and the American Civil War*, Volume 2; (London: Longmans, Green, 1898).

6. Relman Morin, *Dwight D. Eisenhower, A Gauge of Greatness*; (An Associated Press Biography).

7. Carlo D'Este, *Patton – A Genius For War*; (New York: Harper Collins, 1995).

8. Sheila Murray Bethel, *Making A Difference – 12 Qualities That Make You A Leader*; (New York: Berkley Books, 1990).

9. Os Guiness, *Time For Truth*; (Grand Rapids, MI: Baker Books, 2000).

10. Shelton Smith, *The Sword of the Lord*, July14, 2006; (Murfreesboro, TN: Sword of the Lord Publishers).

11. John Wallace, *Control in Conflict*; (Nashville: Broadman Press, 1982).

12. J. Oswald Sanders, *Paul The Leader*; (Colorado Springs, CO: NavPress).

13. Sheila Murray Bethel, *Making A Difference – 12 Qualities That Make You A Leader*; (New York: Berkley Books, 1990).

14. Roger Bruns, Caesar; *World Leaders Past and Present*; (New York: Berkley Books, 1990).

15. Paul Chappell, *Guided by Grace*; (Murfreesboro, TN: Sword of the Lord Publishers, 2000).

16. Os Guiness, *Time For Truth*; (Grand Rapids, MI: Baker Books, 2000).

17. Focus on the Family, Live interview with Michael Reagan, 2004.

18. Ambrose Evans-Pritchard, *The Secret Life of Bill Clinton*: The Unreported Stories; (Washington: Regnery Publishers).

19. Clarence Sexton, *Earnestly Contend For The Faith*; (Powell, TN: Crown Publications, 2001).

20. David J. Vaughan, Statesman and Saint; *The Principled Politics of William Wilberforce*; (Highland Books).

21. Os Guiness, *Time For Truth*; (Grand Rapids, MI: Baker Books, 2000).

22. Robert H. Bork, *Slouching Towards Gomorrah*; (New York, NY: Regan Books/Harper Collins Publishers, 1996).